THE ELITE CONSULTING MIND

THE ELITE CONSULTING MIND

16 Proven Mindsets to Attract More Clients, Increase Your Income, and Achieve Meaningful Success

Michael Zipursky

If you would like further information about Consulting Success or any of our products, programs or services please email info@consultingsuccess.com
Library and Archives Canada Cataloguing in Publication.
Zipursky, Michael, author
The Elite Consulting Mind / Michael Zipursky
ISBN 9781775041108 (Paperback)
1. Consulting. 2. Marketing. 3. Psychology.
ISBN: 1775041107

To my cousin and business partner Sam

TABLE OF CONTENTS

SLEEPLESS NIGHTS

Moonlight through the curtains cast a faint, wavering light on the far wall. It was the middle of the night, and somewhere in the street below, a noise rang out. A clatter, a car door slamming, footsteps on the pavement.

Already wide awake, Beth sat up in bed, her heart racing, and drew the blanket around her. After a moment, she heard the jingle of keys followed by a house door being shut.

She breathed a sigh of relief.

Just the neighbor coming home late. Nothing to worry about.

Beth had tossed and turned for hours, getting no closer to sleep despite all of the effort she'd made to quiet her mind. From time to time, the reflection of headlights raced across the ceiling as cars passed in front of the house. Otherwise, nothing moved except the ceiling fan overhead.

Her husband continued to snore softly beside her, burrowed deep into his pillow. She hadn't spoken to him about her concerns. As far as he knew, her consulting business was still growing and thriving. She'd been tempted to bring it up a few times, but she couldn't do it. She didn't want to see the disappointment on his face.

What do I do? she wondered. *How am I supposed to get my company growing again?*

For the first few years of her business, Beth had experienced some success, bringing in new clients, increasing her revenue, building a reputation in her industry. But somewhere along the way, she'd hit a plateau. Now, she spent every waking hour trying to figure out what had gone wrong, to no avail. She was at her wit's end.

As a result, these restless, interminable nights had become all too common. She dreaded going to bed, knowing that endless wakeful hours awaited her.

In the early days, she'd been full of excitement, ready to talk about her success to anyone who would listen. Now that things had stalled, her world was filled with loneliness and doubt, her mind flooded with worry about the future. Was it the beginning of a downturn?

I don't understand. I'm working as hard as ever, doing all of the things I did at the beginning, all of the things that brought that initial burst of success. Did something change?

Day and night, thoughts raced through her head. There was always something to think about, some problem to wrestle with, some challenge to consider. Quiet moments were the worst.

With a sigh, Beth lay back down in bed, adjusting the covers, and stared up at the ceiling. Another car passed on the street outside, and she watched the headlights move across the room. Suddenly, she felt small and insignificant and utterly alone.

I'm going to fail.

She'd spent twenty years in a billion-dollar company, so she brought a lot of experience to the table. For twenty years, she'd climbed the corporate ladder through hard work and dedication, and after all of that time, she had finally achieved the position of Vice President of Operations.

She'd given it up to start her own consulting business, but she brought the expertise, the knowledge, and the established reputation with her. On paper, she had everything she needed to be successful.

Despite that, her income level had stalled in the last twelve months, and nothing she did helped. She'd tried so many things in an attempt to get the business growing again, but she'd only multiplied her frustration and discouragement.

She still made less money in her consulting business than she'd made in her corporate position, and that didn't seem likely to change. Now, she felt stuck.

It was a failed experiment. She hated that thought, but she couldn't shake it. *You took a risk, started this consulting business, and it didn't work out. That's all there is to it.*

Maybe it was time to slink back to the corporate world with her tail tucked between her legs. She hated the idea of returning to the daily grind of her former career, but she couldn't afford to put it off much longer.

As she lay there for yet another sleepless night, she considered the possibility of trying to get her old job back. She needed the money, and she needed the consistency. Most of all, she needed to be able to sleep again.

I wonder if my old boss would hire me back? I left on fairly good terms. Maybe if I grovel.

THE WRONG MINDSET

Beth's story is not unique. She has the experience, she's accepted the risks, and she's thrown everything she has into becoming a successful consultant. She had some success early on, and that filled her with hope for the future. But somewhere along the way, her business has stopped growing, and she can't figure out why. The things that brought her success before no longer seem to work.

So many independent consultants and owners of small consulting firms find themselves in a similar situation.

It's a frustrating place to be. Many struggling consultants feel alone because they lack a support network to provide encouragement and advice. They might speak openly to a spouse or loved one about their business, but inwardly they still have many doubts.

Why can't I achieve a greater level of success? I can't figure out what I'm doing wrong.

Is that your story?

For the last eighteen years, I've built successful consulting businesses, coaching and working with hundreds of consultants from around the world. I've seen what they struggle with. I've discussed their frustrations and fears. This has given me a unique perspective on what consultants deal with on a daily basis.

If you're struggling to achieve greater success, you need to understand that you are far from alone. I encounter the same themes over and over. Consultants tend to have the same questions, the same challenges and frustrations, whether they are leading a firm or running a solo business.

In the end, many of these recurring issues can be traced back to a single common source: the consultant's mindset.

That includes you. I haven't heard your story yet, but it's likely that your mindset is a major contributing cause of your current struggles.

The wrong mindset becomes a hindrance to success. It holds people back and prevents them from achieving the breakthrough that they dream of. I've seen it too many times to dismiss the connection. A single thought might seem insignificant compared to the larger picture, but how you choose to deal with that thought really does lay the groundwork for success or failure in your business.

Is it possible you've been defeating yourself with your own mindset? Is it possible the way you deal with nagging thoughts is creating roadblocks in your path?

Think of it this way. Every professional boxer gets knocked down from time to time, even the best of them. Possibly the greatest prize fighter of all time, Muhammad Ali, had an impressive record of fifty-six wins and five losses, but he still got knocked down a few times over the course of his career.

One of the most dramatic examples happened during his first fight with Henry Cooper in June 1963 in front of thirty-five thousand spectators. Ali hadn't expected much from Cooper, saying before the fight, "I'm not even worried about this big bum." However, Cooper turned out to be a much more skillful and dangerous opponent that he anticipated, holding his own for five brutal rounds.

The most dramatic moment happened in Round 4, when Ali took a fierce left hook to the jaw. He fell back against the ropes and slid down to the mat, dazed. A bell ended the round shortly thereafter, and Ali stumbled to his corner.

Many boxers would have been shaken by the experience, but Ali came back in the fifth round with renewed energy. It was a literal bloodbath. After a flurry of fierce punches from both men, Cooper received a deep cut above his left eye. It bled so profusely that judges stopped the fight and awarded the victory to Muhammad Ali.

When he faced Henry Cooper again in 1966, he'd learned how to counter him and fought smarter. Interviewed shortly before the second fight, Ali told the British press, "No man knocks me down and gets away with it, so you be ready for it, you hear?" This time, they went six rounds before Ali again opened a large gash over Cooper's left eye, a cut that required sixteen stitches. Judges ended the fight in Ali's favor.

Nobody would dare to call Muhammad Ali a failure for getting knocked down by Henry Cooper. He got back up again, he fought on, and he learned from the experience. That, ultimately, is the key to success. When you fall, you don't stay down. You pick yourself up, learn and adjust, strengthen yourself, and return to the fight more determined than ever.

I speak from experience. In fact, I've had more than the typical mental challenges to overcome in my life. You see, I suffer from a condition called Idiopathic Hypersomnia. It's a condition I haven't told many people about, but it has required hours and hours of research, nights at the lab, blood work, and visits to multiple doctors and specialists.

You know how when you go to sleep, you wake up in the morning feeling refreshed? You recall how good it feels after a long, hard day at work to lie down and get seven or eight hours of solid sleep? It recharges your battery, and all of the exhaustion just goes away. With my condition, that doesn't happen. No matter how long I sleep, my battery never gets fully charged.

People with Idiopathic Hypersomnia often feel excessively sleepy all the time. Can you imagine how crippling that could be, especially when you're trying to build a business? There's no cure for it, and the cause remains unknown. Prescription drugs have been recommended, but I'm not a fan of them. I'd rather not deal with the side effects.

So what do I do? Well, if I wanted, I could let it be an excuse. Nobody would blame me for slowing down a little. My body is often exhausted and would love nothing more than to crawl back into bed and pull the sheets over my head. My mind won't allow it. I won't allow it. I have a family to care for and clients to serve, so I push myself. I get up at 5am, make myself exercise every day, and somehow run two successful businesses.

I wouldn't want it any other way.

The reason I share this with you is because when I talk about having the right mindset, overcoming challenges, self-doubts, and struggles, I speak from experience. I achieved success in the face of an overwhelming personal challenge, while still navigating the typical struggles that everyone deals with. I'm no superhuman. I got there through hard work and the right mindset, so I know you can, too.

WHY I WROTE *THE ELITE CONSULTING MIND*

In this book, I want to give you some of the tools you need to keep moving toward greater success. I'm going to share with you real stories of people who have struggled and achieved their dreams. I'll answer some of the common questions and deal with some of the common challenges that consultants like you deal with every day. In the end, you'll see how a shift in your mindset can help you overcome the obstacles you're facing.

I know these lessons and mindset changes work because they've made the difference in my consulting career. In my early twenties, I was consulting for billion-dollar companies, and by age thirty-two, I'd become a millionaire. Since then, I've continued to sharpen my mindset and hone my skills in order to achieve more growth for my clients, my team, and the companies I run, and I've never looked back.

Some of the stories I'll share with you come from our own clients. For the sake of privacy, I've changed the names of the clients whose stories I share. Many of them, after coming to us discouraged and frustrated, are now enjoying tremendous success, more than they ever dreamed possible.

With our help, and their commitment and determination, they are working with clients they love, taking on exciting projects, earning greater income than they ever imagined, and enjoying far more freedom and flexibility than they had in the corporate world.

I want that to be your story as well. Whatever challenges you've faced, whatever frustrations you've experienced in trying to grow your business, I am confident that you are on the cusp of greater things. I believe that breakthrough success is possible because I've seen it in our own businesses and with so many of our clients. The journey that you are about to begin in this book will give you a real advantage in your consulting business and in your life. By properly applying the principles I'm going to share, you will experience more success than you ever thought possible.

Are you ready? Let's go!

1

MINDSET, ACTION, RESULTS

David seemed frustrated, fiddling with the pencils and pens at the edge of his desk. Sunlight from a small window cast his shadow across the desk and up the far wall. His office was modest, a spare bedroom at the back of his house. I heard his children laughing and playing in another room nearby.

"I'm getting impatient," he said. "I'm ready to take my business to the next level, but I can't seem to get it there. I thought I'd be farther along by now."

As he spoke, I noticed the corner of a folded piece of notebook paper sticking out of his shirt pocket. I gestured at it.

"You made some notes?" I asked.

He grabbed the piece of paper. "I know what I need to do, but it's just not happening."

He unfolded the piece of paper and set it on the desk. At the top of the page, he'd written the words "Action" and "Result" in blue ink. Beneath the word "Result," he'd written "More clients." He pointed at this.

"That's the key to growth, right?" he said. "I need more clients."

"That's part of it," I replied. "More clients, especially higher-value clients."

Beneath the word "Action," he'd written, "More outreach and follow-up calls." He tapped this with a finger.

"And that's what I need to do, right?"

"There is definitely no substitute for having real conversations with prospective buyers," I said. "How many conversations have you had with prospective buyers this week?"

David sighed and grabbed the piece of paper, refolding it and tucking it back into his shirt pocket.

"It seems so easy when I write it down," he said. "I tried to follow up with a potential client named Susan this morning. I sent her an email about my consulting services last week, and I just need to make sure she read it."

"How did it go?"

David resumed fiddling with a pen, picking it up and tapping it on the desk before putting it back down again.

"I get butterflies every time I start dialing her number," he said. "It doesn't seem like such a big deal to follow up with a client...until I try to do it."

"So what happened?"

He sighed. "I hung up before the first ring. I just wasn't in the right mood for it. Nobody wants a phone call first thing in the morning. Plus, I don't have a good introduction worked out yet."

"So it's the introduction that you feel is holding you back?" I asked.

He shrugged. "Maybe I'll try again this evening. She'll be home from work, probably relaxing and in a better mood."

He leaned back in his chair.

"David, what you've written on that piece of paper isn't bad," I said. "It's just missing the first step, and until you address the first step, it will never be the right day, or the right time of day, and your introduction will never seem good enough."

David gave me a confused look. Clearly, this was not what he'd expected to hear.

"Identifying the actions you need to take to get the result you want is important," I said. "But we need to address what's holding you back from ultimately taking action."

THE FIRST STEP

David's experience is common to consultants. What might not be so obvious is where his problem begins. After all, David is doing what most people do when they're trying to

3

grow their business. He is clarifying the result he wants and identifying the action it will take to get there.

It makes sense, which is why most people follow the same pattern. In my experience, most entrepreneurs spend the bulk of their time thinking and planning this way. They get coaching to help them figure it out, read books and articles, all in an effort to identify the best actions.

As I told David, this "action/result" paradigm is missing its first and most important step. If you really want to achieve the best possible result, there is something you must work on before you figure out what action to take.

Only a few people have the natural boldness to immediately implement their plan. Most people, particularly when confronting some new challenge, will hit roadblocks, most of which are internal.

The problem has to do with mindset. When you take action, especially when you're heading into uncharted territory, you suddenly find yourself beyond calm waters.

As in the case of David, he knows what he needs to do: he needs to follow up with some potential clients. However, this is not something he's comfortable with, and perhaps it's something he's never really done before. It's not as easy as picking up the phone and dialing the number.

What's the primary roadblock for David? Fear. New actions in uncharted territory are often steeped in fear. Unfortunately, a lot of new consultants don't anticipate the

The Elite Consulting Mind

fear when they make plans, so when they run into it for the first time, maybe as they are just about to call a new client, they don't know how to deal with it.

Whether you're making a direct sale or just confirming that a client got an email you sent them, those direct connections are intimidating.

In the planning stages, it seems so simple.

"Start calling people. Start winning new clients."

Action and result. Then you try to dial that number, and you feel the butterflies in your stomach. Suddenly, it becomes really easy to set the phone aside and delay, delay, delay.

What solves the problem? The right mindset. Before you start planning actions and thinking about results, you have to develop the right mindset. A successful consultant has already convinced himself or herself of the true importance of making that phone call before they dial the number. They've settled in their mind what needs to be done, and they've mentally prepared themselves for it.

Most coaches focus on actions and results. They sit down with the consultant and ask them, "Okay, what result do you want? What level of success? What income level would you like to achieve?" And once the consultant has identified those things, the coach says, "Now, let's figure out what you need to do to achieve them."

They might come up with an elaborate list of actions, but because they are starting at the wrong place, they are setting consultants up for constant frustration and ultimate disappointment.

It's a little like trying to climb a mountain for the first time. Suppose a young woman is determined to conquer her first peak. She sits down with an experienced climber, and she pours over a map of the mountain.

Together, they discuss all the possible routes to the top and work out the best and fastest way to ascend. She studies the map and memorizes her path until she knows every step along the way by heart. The expert shows her the technical aspects of climbing, making sure she understands the process in depth. He makes sure she has a good set of climbing shoes, demonstrates how to use the carabiner and harness, and helps her practice with the belay device until she's got it down.

"You know every action you need to take," he says, finally. "Now, go climb the mountain. Good luck."

When she's finally standing at the bottom, gazing up at the mountaintop a few thousand feet above her, she feels a little flutter in her stomach, but it's not bad.

It's seems higher than I thought it would, but I know every step to get to the top.

And then she starts to climb. Even though she memorized the map, she quickly learns that the actual experience

The Elite Consulting Mind

of climbing is much different than staring at a map. By the time she's twenty feet off the ground, the flutter has turned into stomach-churning anxiety.

Wow, it's a lot more intense than I expected, she thinks, glancing down at the ground. *And it seems a lot harder.*

Indeed, every time she reaches up for a new handhold, she feels a burst of fear. The expert she consulted didn't really prepare her for how paralyzing the fear would be. After forty feet, every movement becomes a challenge.

She shuts her eyes and remembers the map, tracing out the path again in her head. She can see it so clearly. Every single twist and turn in her path to the top. It's all there. But when she opens her eyes and tries to move, her hands are shaking and her whole body trembles.

Maybe I'll just hang out here at this spot on the mountain for a while, she thinks. *I'm forty feet up. The rope is firmly in place. I can just chill out and wait for the fear to pass.*

So she settles in, but the longer she stays there, the less likely it seems that she'll ever reach the peak. In fact, as time passes, even taking that next step begins to feel impossible.

It's not a lack of knowledge holding her back. She sees the actions she needs to take to reach her goal, but fear and uncertainty are holding her back. She needs a new mindset to help her take action.

To get a certain result, creating the right mindset is always the first step. Mindset, Action, Result. That's the proper order. Sadly, few consultants spend a lot of time adjusting their way of thinking before taking action. This is especially true for independent consultants who work by themselves or with a small staff, since they lack opportunity to discuss plans with others.

If you develop the right mindset, you will be able to take action more readily, overcome challenges and fears, and get real results. What does this look like in practice?

Instead of figuring out what actions you need to take in order grow your business, take a look at yourself and figure out what actions you have a hard time carrying out. What are the things that you aren't doing that you know you should be doing?

Once you've identified those things, get to the root of the fear. Maybe, like David, it's calling on potential clients. Ask yourself, what's the worst thing that could happen when you take that action?

When you've figured out why a certain action is so hard for you then you can determine how to make it easier. You are laying the groundwork so that once you know what you need to do, you will have fewer mental roadblocks about doing it.

As you start making progress, it becomes easier to take action. Success has a way of emboldening people. But until you get there, it's going to be easy to give up, and if you don't experience success right away, if you have a few missteps at first, a few negative experiences, it can create more roadblocks in your mind.

A homerun champion doesn't knock it out of the park on his first time up to bat. Instead, he gets there after years of preparation and training, developing the skills and the right mindset to step up to the plate and swing away.

It's no simple thing to stand in front of thousands of screaming fans, with a whole team counting on you, and hit that ninety-mile-an-hour fastball. Skill alone isn't enough. The player must be mentally prepared.

Even so, the best players don't hit a homerun every time they're up to bat. Sometimes they strike out, but they have the mindset to take it in stride and try again.

"I struck out, but next time, I'm going to send it out of the park!"

It's a mindset that prepares even the best baseball player for the next opportunity, helps them bounce back from a loss and achieve their peak performance.

It's the mindset of successful people. Make it your mindset, and you'll start to grow.

MINDSET REVIEW

- Your mindset is the biggest factor in determining your success.

- Focusing on actions and results is important, but if you don't have the right mindset you'll take less action which will lead to fewer results.

- Acquiring knowledge is also important, but it doesn't replace taking action.

- The more action you take, the more you'll encounter personal hindrances which provide opportunities for you to learn how to deal with them and move forward.

- If taking a certain action is hard for you, figure out why, so you can determine how to make it easier.

2

CONFIDENCE CREATES SUCCESS

His stomach in knots, a trickle of sweat running down the back of his neck, Cory pushed the door open and stepped into the conference room. A large table dominated the room, and suddenly he felt small and out of his element. His hands were hot and sweaty, his heart racing, all symptoms he hoped the prospective buyer wouldn't notice.

Look professional, he chided himself. *Don't let him see how nervous you are.*

But he had so many questions, so many doubts.

Will he compare me to other consultants he's spoken to? Will I sound like an expert?

His consulting business hadn't been around long, only a matter of months, so he didn't have the years of experience or the vast client list that others had. Would it show?

He approached the large table in the middle of the room, as the prospective buyer rose on the other side to greet him. They shook hands briefly, Cory hoping his hand wasn't too damp. Was the buyer's smile genuine? Was that a glimmer of doubt in his eye?

Is he already judging me? Is he already having second thoughts?

As he sat down, he cleared his throat and tried to think of something to say, something that would make him sound confident.

Across the country, another consultant named John was having a different challenge. He'd experienced some success already, growing his business to a couple hundred thousand dollars a year. He had a lot to be proud of, a lot to be excited about, but recent developments had sent him into a panic.

His business depended largely on referrals and his own network, and for a while, this had been a good thing. He'd had a steady stream of clients, and he hadn't had to worry about where his next prospect would come from. However, in the last four years, the referral well had begun to dry up, and now, as pressure mounted, he had no new business in sight.

The well had finally gone dry.

What do I do next? John wondered.

He had heard people talking about the power of paid advertising, so that felt like the right way to go. He did his research first, reading articles on how to create effective ads. He even took a course on the latest social media tactics.

As he worked through the course, he couldn't shake the feeling that while this approach was popular and many people were talking about it, it didn't feel right for the type of corporate client he was going after.

He finally sat down to create his own ads, but it was a struggle. Nothing he came up with satisfied him. He had so much self-doubt.

Nobody's going to respond, he thought. *I'm wasting time and money making these ads. People will scroll right past them without a second thought.*

He kept fiddling with them, making adjustments, rewording the ad copy in a hundred different ways. No matter what he did, he didn't feel confident.

I don't sound like an expert. My ideal client won't be impressed.

Finally, he just sat there at his desk, staring at nothing in particular. He felt like a boat out at sea on a windy day. He was being tossed back and forth with no clear direction. He had no idea how to navigate his way back to shore. With every passing day, the anxiety built.

I have to figure something out, he thought. *It can't keep going this way.*

THE BIGGEST ROADBLOCK

Cory and John come from different backgrounds, and they're working in different industries. Their situations don't seem to have much in common, but, in reality, they are both dealing with the same core problem: a lack of confidence.

It's the single biggest problem that consultants deal with, and the single biggest roadblock to success.

"Am I good enough?"

"Can I call myself an expert?"

"Are my fees too high? Maybe I'm not worth that much money."

"What happens if I say or do the wrong thing?"

Do you ask yourself these kinds of questions? Maybe they're running through your head all the time, a constant internal monologue of self-doubt. Maybe they go through your mind when you're meeting with a prospective buyer, trying to create marketing materials, or when you're staring at the phone and thinking about making a call.

Your lack of confidence is a hindrance to your consulting business. Why? Because it causes you to second-guess yourself. It prevents you from taking bold steps and results in inaction.

That lack of action, in turn, causes your lack of confidence to increase, so it becomes an endless cycle. Put another way, you'd have more confidence if you took action, but you don't take action because you lack confidence. It's like a car stuck in the mud. Desperate to move forward, the driver guns the engine. The wheels are spinning, churning up a lot of mud, but the car doesn't go anywhere. After a while, the driver begins to believe he'll never get the car out, and when despair sets in, he gradually gives up. Finally, he's just sitting there behind the steering wheel, staring through a mud-speckled windshield at the road ahead of him, a road he can't seem to get down.

Have you felt like this in your business?

Where does confidence come from? It comes from knowing what to do and doing it. That sounds simple enough, doesn't it? Yet we often struggle. It's not simply about taking action. More than that, it's about taking the right action. Specifically, it's about taking an action that will move you closer to the outcome or goal you want.

You want your business to become more financially successful? Take action in ways that move you closer to that goal. When you do that, it's called progress. Think about being a runner in a race. Every step you take moves you closer to the finish line, but only as long as you are stepping in the right direction. How do you finish the race? By continuing to make progress in the right direction.

If you're running a long race, the finish line can seem like it's far away, but there's no trick to it. Just start taking steps in that direction. As you do that, you will pass mile markers along the way, and with each one of those, your confidence about reaching the finish line will grow.

What if you're running a race, and you get turned around? Maybe it's a marathon through the streets of a big city, and you take a wrong turn. Suddenly, you're taking steps that aren't getting you closer to the finish line. They might even be taking you farther away. What can you do when that happens?

There's really only one option. Turn around, reorient yourself toward the finish line, and resume moving in the right direction. You'll still finish the race, it might just take a little longer. At the same time, maybe you'll figure out how you got turned around, so you're less likely to do it again. You've learned something.

In the same way, if you've taken an action or made a decision in your business that turned out to be a mistake, receive it as a learning experience. Figure out why it didn't work and what you could've done better.

Once you've identified what doesn't work, you're closer to figuring out what does. Reorient yourself toward your goal and move in that direction. The last thing you want to do is let the discouragement get to you. Learn from it and take smarter action in the future.

Need more confidence? The progress you make from taking the action boosts confidence. Like that runner, the closer you get to the finish line, the more confident you become that you'll get there. That's why runners often get a second wind late into a long race.

The key to success, then, is taking action. The more action you take, the more successful you will be. When you make mistakes, you learn from it, and that increases your ability to take the right action in the future. In other words, you become more competent.

Success increases as a direct result of two things: confidence and competence. Both of these increase as you take action.

Now, let's take all of that and apply it to those nagging questions of self-doubt. Here's how you need to deal with each one of them, and why it's important that you do so right away.

"Am I good enough?"

Here's an easy way to answer this question. Look at your own experience. How many years have you worked in your field? Five, ten, twenty? While you can't replace the benefits that come from years of experience, what's most important is the value you deliver to clients. Buyers aren't paying you for experience. They are paying you for results. That's where your focus should be.

Have you been able to create results and provide value for your clients and employees? If your answer is yes, then it's time to stop doubting yourself. You've already proved that you're good enough to people along the way. Even taking into account your mistakes and failures, you've already demonstrated your worth. Stop doubting and start believing in yourself.

"Can I call myself an expert?"

An expert is defined as "a person who has comprehensive and authoritative knowledge of or a skill in a particular area," and authoritative is defined as "able to be trusted as being accurate or true; reliable." Put in simplest terms, if you know your stuff and can provide value and results for your clients, or if you've done so in the past, then you can honestly call yourself an expert. And you should, boldly and confidently.

"Can I ask for higher fees?"

The simple fact that you're asking this question means the answer is almost certainly, "Yes." You're asking because you sense that you aren't getting what you're worth. You aren't earning the value for what you provide clients. If that wasn't the case, the question wouldn't be nagging you constantly.

The real question is why are you charging so little for what you have to offer? Why haven't you already raised your fees? Something must be holding you back. A little later, we'll revisit this issue. It needs to be addressed in depth because it's such a problem for consultants.

"What happens if I do or say the wrong thing?"

Every mistake you make is a chance to learn, and the more you learn, the easier it is to make the right decision or take the right action in the future. If you say the wrong thing to a client, you'll know not to say it again. If you make a decision that hurts your business, you'll know to do things differently in the future.

What you mustn't do is let your mistakes bog you down. Don't let your regret over past mistakes prevent you from taking action in the future. You know what's worse than making a mistake? Doing nothing. When you do something wrong, try to learn from it and keep moving forward. Never let fear hold you back. Go for it!

EMBRACING MISTAKES

Consider the career of Walt Disney. Everyone now knows the company he founded, which bears his name. It's one of the largest and most successful companies in the world, but Walt had a series of notable failures before he found success.

His dream was to create a successful animation company, but his first two attempts utterly failed. He started the first company, Laugh-O-Gram Studio, in Kansas City in 1920 with a friend and fellow animator Ub Iwerks. They began creating short animated films for local theaters, but they couldn't seem to turn a profit.

Soon enough, the company was struggling to make ends meet, and Disney had no money for rent or food. He took to living in his office, but it wasn't enough. Laugh-O-Gram filed for bankruptcy in 1923.

Despite this embarrassing failure, Walt Disney was undeterred. He packed up a cardboard suitcase and headed to California, intending to try again, this time with the help of his brother Roy. Together, they formed Disney Brothers Studio and put together a small team of animators.

The company found modest success with a cartoon character named Oswald the Lucky Rabbit. Unfortunately, in 1928, Disney's distributor, Charles Mintz, stole the rights to the character right out from under his nose. He also hired away most of his animators. Walt found out during a train ride back from New York City that he'd lost everything once again.

Most people would have given up at this point. How many complete failures, after all, can a person be expected to endure? But Walt Disney had a stubborn determination to succeed, and he kept trying. His next creation proved to be his breakthrough, a little cartoon mouse named Mickey that he designed with the help of his old friend Ub Iwerks.

This time, instead of being more cautious, Walt decided to take an even bigger risk. He converted one of the first Mickey Mouse cartoons into the first sound cartoon, an innovation that required more money, which made it an even bigger gamble. Needless to say, that first cartoon, *Steamboat Willie*, was a historic success, and Mickey Mouse quickly became popular with children across the country and around the world.

In fact, it didn't take long for Mickey Mouse to become the most recognized fictional character in the world, and even today, you'd be hard-pressed to find a single person who doesn't know the name or recognize the face. Few people in Walt's position would have endured long enough to have enjoyed the success of Mickey Mouse.

What did he have that others lack? How did he absorb such big failures and still keep striving, innovating, and working hard? He had a mindset to succeed, even in the face of crushing disappointment. He learned from his failures, adjusted, and kept fighting toward his goal.

Sir James Dyson, the famous British inventor, struggled for years before finding success. In fact, the bagless vacuum cleaner that ultimately propelled him to success was the result of thousands of failed prototypes in a grueling process that lasted five years. However, each new prototype brought him a step closer to his breakthrough, and he believed in his product enough to keep trying.

When the product was finally perfected, he had trouble getting it into the market. Major manufacturers didn't want it. Eventually, after creating his own manufacturing company, his bagless vacuum cleaner hit the UK market, and it quickly became a huge hit.

Since then, he's gone on to invent other successful products, including the Dyson Airblade hand dryer, and the success has made him a billionaire. But he never would have enjoyed that success if he hadn't endured the years of hardship, mistakes, and learning.

Successful people learn from their mistakes and keep moving toward their goal with confidence in their own potential. Follow their examples.

MINDSET REVIEW

- If you doubt yourself and lack confidence, your business will suffer. It's normal to have questions and doubts as you build your business, but don't let them hold you back. Take bold action.

- Don't worry about making mistakes. Once you've identified what doesn't work, you're closer to figuring out what does.

- True buyers engage you for the results you can deliver and the outcome you will provide, not your degree, appearance, or years of experience.

- As long as you can deliver value and results for clients, consider yourself an expert.

- Almost every successful entrepreneur has failed, in some cases many times, before they achieved real success. Don't let fear of failure deter you.

3

EARNING PREMIUM FEES

The bright morning sun cast long shadows down the street and across the parking lot. The clock on the dashboard read, "8:00AM," as I pulled into a parking space and killed the engine. As I stepped out of the car, I smelled the salt air and saw the ocean waves, sparkling silver from the sun's thousand reflections.

The Pan Pacific Hotel rose up before me, a bright, white edifice against the water. I entered the lobby and moved past the massive, granite check-in desk, heading up a flight of stairs toward the restaurant on the second floor.

Despite the early hour, the restaurant was packed, men and women in suits and skirts huddled around tables, only half-interested in the plates of food set before them. It was an industry conference, and there was business to discuss, connections to make, and stories to swap.

I picked out Denise on the far side of the room, the only person sitting alone. She was there for the industry conference just like all of the others, but she was also in town to meet with me. Her body posture, her hands flipping through a small stack of papers in front of her, made her appear nervous, overwhelmed.

I'd spoken to her on the phone, but this was the first time we met in person. For some reason, she was seated at a rather large table, and it dwarfed her. As I approached, she continued to fumble through the papers, and now I could see her mouth moving. Practicing her speech.

Once I got close, she spotted me and attempted a smile. I saw the anxiety behind it. She rose from the table, and we shook hands. Her handshake felt weak and uncertain, half-committed.

I wasn't surprised. I've seen it more times than I can count. Denise was giving a presentation at the conference, and, like most people, she was nervous, running through the words in her head, afraid she'd get up in front of all of those people and her mind would go blank.

She'd invited me to the hotel so I could review her notes. As I sat across the oversized table from her, she slid the small stack of pages toward me, and I reviewed them briefly.

The speech was fine. I gave her a few tips to clarify some of her points before sliding the notes back over. That wasn't what I really wanted to talk about. I was more concerned about the well-being of her consulting business.

Finally, I asked for her latest revenue and pipeline numbers, so we could spend a few minutes reviewing her marketing plan.

"Well, I have two new opportunities, Michael," she said.

I asked for specifics. What are the opportunities? What will she be charging?

At the second question, the tone of the conversation changed. Denise bit her lip, suddenly reluctant to speak. I felt the tension.

"How will you structure your fees for these engagements?" I asked again.

She cleared her throat and responded.

"Michael, you won't be happy with me," she said. "I'm thinking about charging them an hourly fee."

I asked for specific numbers, and she finally gave them to me. As I suspected, the numbers were way too low. She wasn't charging even close to what she was worth, and she knew it.

"Denise, why are you charging so little?" I asked. "You bring a lot more value to the projects than this."

The answer she gave me is an answer I hear often.

"It's what I thought they would pay."

I wonder if this is happening to you. Are you charging far less than you should for your consulting services? It seems hard to ask for more money, but it really isn't. You just need to know how to approach it effectively.

There are two essential parts to charging higher fees. First, you have to know how to effectively raise your fees. Second, you must have the confidence to ask for more money. We'll take a look at both of them.

In Denise's case, I had already spoken to her on the phone about raising her fees. I'd coached her through asking for more money, and she was able to do it with me on the phone. The problem was that she lacked the confidence to do it with clients.

YOU DESERVE MORE

Yes, we're back to the issue of self-confidence. A lack of confidence is the number one enemy in the world of consulting, but if you're struggling to make ends meet, the fastest and most effective way to earn greater income as a consultant is to increase your fees. Chances are you're making less than you could be simply because you lack the confidence to ask for it.

There came a point in my own consulting business where we finally decided to pull the trigger. We planned on increasing our fees by fifty percent. That's a huge increase, but I knew we were worth it. We'd provided value for our clients, and they were getting great results and ROI on their investment. We'd held back far too long.

What finally brought us to the decision point was a conversation I had with a business professional that I knew. He was curious about what I did as a consultant, so I explained the business and shared how we helped other consultants to grow. He then asked me for my rates. When I told him, his eyes widened.

"That's amazing," he said. "Your fees are so reasonable. I think you could charge a lot more."

That comment stuck with me, and it was the thing that finally settled the issue in my mind. It was time to charge what our services were worth.

That afternoon, we made the decision to increase our fees by fifty percent, and the next day, we got our first new client at the higher rate. The client didn't balk or complain. They recognized the value of the services we were providing and agreed to it.

Nothing had changed about the way we did business, the way we delivered our services, or what we provided. We simply recognized that our clients saw great results, that their businesses had benefited from our work, and that they experienced amazing ROI.

Increasing fees by fifty percent might seem extreme, but it was never an issue with any of our clients. In fact, many of them have successfully increased their fees by a hundred, two hundred, or three hundred percent. One client even increased her fees by seven hundred percent. As long as buyers can see the value in your services, as long as ROI is still significant for them, they will pay what you ask. It's a win-win.

That single change added over a million dollars to our bottom line, and we've continued to increase our fees every six months ever since.

I talk at length about how to charge higher consulting fees in my book *Consulting Success System*. For now, we'll focus our discussion on developing the right mindset for success.

An unhealthy mindset is a major contributing factor to many consultants undercharging for their services. Like Denise, they worry about prospective buyers turning them down.

"Your fees are too high! Forget it. I refuse to pay that much. Who do you think you are charging such exorbitant rates?"

In fact, Denise told me she always knew she was worth more. What prevented her from asking for more? A lack of confidence, of course. Though she had a higher fee in mind, self-doubt prevented her from going for it.

"The buyer will say no. They'll go with another consultant. I'm not really worth that much to them."

It's a particular struggle for early-stage consultants. They worry that they don't have enough experience to charge premium fees. My response to such clients is to change their focus. Quit focusing on what the buyer already has. Focus on what they want.

Sure, the buyer might be older than you. They might have more money than you. They might run a larger company than you. But do they have the same level of expertise as you in the area that they want to engage you in? It's likely they don't. Otherwise, they wouldn't be talking to you in the first place.

The buyer is aware of their own lack, and they've seen the value of what you have to offer. Even though they have all of that other stuff, they don't have what you're offering, and that's what they want.

You might be new to consulting, but you are not new to your area of expertise. That's what brought you into this business in the first place, isn't it? You have a strong level of expertise to offer.

Remember, in the buyer's mind, you're the expert. Are you the number one expert in the world? Maybe not yet. However, you are still an expert to your client, and that means you can charge expert fees.

The moment you decide to increase your fees is the same moment you can start to earn those higher fees.

Can it really be that straightforward?

After eighteen years of building successful consulting businesses and coaching hundreds of consultants from around the world, I can say with confidence, "Yes, it's that straightforward."

However, your mind is going to create all kinds of reasons why you shouldn't increase your fees.

"I need to wait a little longer before I do it."

"Things need to be aligned better before I take that step."

Don't listen to these thoughts. As long as you can provide significant value and ROI for the buyer, you can and should command premium fees. Make the change today, right now, at this exact moment.

Just think about how dramatically higher fees will change your business and your life. It will mean you can work with fewer clients to hit your target income. That will allow you to be more present, more focused, and more engaged with each client, which means you'll be able to serve each and every client at the highest level.

But what about those clients you're already working with? You can't suddenly charge higher fees with an existing client, can you? After all, you've already offered them a lower rate.

This is a common mindset block. My response? Don't let history dictate your future.

Your existing clients are already familiar with a little thing called inflation. Every year, prices go up. They pay more for a pair of shoes or a hamburger this year than they did five years ago. They pay more for their utilities than they did in the past. In fact, prices increase regularly for almost every product or service that people buy. Why should your business be any different?

If a bread company can charge more for the same loaf of bread this year than they did a few years ago, why can't you charge more for your services? It's normal for consultants to increase their prices at least once a year, if not several times a year. Why? Because your skills and experience are growing, your level of expertise is increasing. As you deliver more value and greater results for clients, often in a shorter period of time, your fees can and should increase.

I've seen many clients transform their consulting businesses just by making this one change. I encouraged one of my clients, Sonaya, to improve her pricing structure in such a way that her fees increased by forty percent. The immediate effect?

In her own words, "I've already landed two new projects at my new rate."

The overall effect?

"I've doubled my business in less than twelve weeks."

Another client, Amir, made a dramatic increase in revenue simply by dropping his hourly rate. In his own words, "I charged high fees by the hour and thought it was smart. Two brief conversations with Michael changed that. I realized I was in fact limiting my ability to grow and potentially work with bigger corporate clients. As a result, a whole new world of possibilities opened up to me and led me on a journey that's helped me grow both personally and professionally."

Theirs are not isolated stories. I've seen these kinds of results with many clients. So why are you still holding back? Why are you letting self-doubt prevent you from taking this essential step? Don't wait another day, another hour, another minute to raise your fees.

MINDSET REVIEW

- Chances are you're making less than you could be simply because you lack the confidence to ask for more.

- Don't base your fees on what you see in the market or what others have done before you. Your fees should be based on the ROI and value you can deliver to clients.

- It's easy to find reasons to hold off increasing your fees, but the moment you decide to ask for more is the moment you'll start earning more.

4

FACING THE UNCOMFORTABLE

Two factors fight against your progress: fear and the uncomfortable. Fear rears its head in many ways that we'll discuss throughout this book. For now, let's take a look at how the uncomfortable stands in your way.

Consider the story of Martin, a client of mine who confronted the uncomfortable and overcame it.

I scheduled a coaching call with Martin one warm summer day, and, as I often do, I found a nice place in my backyard to make the call. I sat on the steps of the wooden deck beside the pond, enjoying the warm sun, the cloudless blue sky mirrored in the still surface of the water. Hummingbirds danced among the flowers at the base of the trees, as I dialed Martin's number.

Though I knew he kept his phone with him, it took three rings before he answered.

"Hello?" A hesitant greeting. What was that edge in his voice?

"How's it going, Martin?"

"Oh, it's going really good, Michael," he replied.

"Hey, I'd love to get an update from you on the progress you've made since we last spoke," I said. "Then we can go over any questions you might have, and we'll work through and update the plan together."

"Well…" Martin started to answer, hesitated a moment, and continued. "Honestly, I haven't made as much progress as I'd like."

He went on to tell me that he'd tried to work through the items we'd discussed in our previous talk.

"I spent a lot of time thinking about who to contact," he said. "I reviewed the website content, too, but…" He cleared his throat. "I'm not sure about a few things."

Whatever was going on with Martin, he didn't want to talk about it. It took some poking and prodding to get to the root of the problem. Eventually, I had to go through the list with him point by point, and only then did it become clear what he'd done and failed to do. It also became clear to me what was really going on, and it's a problem that many consultants face.

Martin came from a corporate background. His former position had always dictated what was expected of him and what he was supposed to do. He'd had multiple levels of accountability with a team of people surrounding him to ensure he got things done.

But he'd left the corporate world to become a consultant, and now it was just him and his business partner working together. As they ramped up their consulting business, Martin began shying away from some of the activities that are critical to growing a business, particularly the things he wasn't comfortable with and didn't enjoy. Since he no longer had multiple people holding him accountable, it became easy for him to avoid these things. Nobody was going to scold him for it. Nobody on his staff was checking up on him regularly.

Martin is not alone. Most people, when presented with the option to do either familiar, comfortable things or new, uncomfortable things, will default to the former.

WASTED HOURS

Every day, you get to choose what you work on. Either you fill the day with easy activities, or you challenge yourself, reach out, and take risks. When nobody is standing over your shoulder to hold you accountable, it becomes far too easy to avoid the risks.

The truth is, you can waste many hours working on your website, tweaking your social media profiles, researching a new service or technology, or updating a presentation that you might give in the future. These are all easy tasks. They don't require any risk or challenge.

Unfortunately, they also don't do much to grow your business, even if they are sometimes necessary. What really brings in new clients and new revenue are the things that people often avoid like the plague: picking up the phone to follow up with a prospective client, sending them a letter or email, writing to the editor of a trade publication, creating a brand-new piece of thought leadership content. All of these things are also challenging.

How long have you been putting them off?

When nobody is forcing you to pick up that phone and dial those numbers, it's tempting to avoid doing it. The problem is, a lot of what you spend your days doing, the comfortable work you focus on, is hindering your progress and, quite frankly, wasting time.

But it's worse than that. The comfortable activities can actually create a false sense of progress, and this is detrimental to your mindset.

Your mind plays tricks on you.

You spend eight hours tweaking design aspects of your website, and at the end of the day, your mind says, "Wow, good job! We really worked hard today. We accomplished a lot." And the truth is, you did nothing to advance your business.

Your mind will also make excuses to keep putting off the uncomfortable work.

"No, no, we can't call that prospective client today. We have to finish the website first. Once we get the website in good shape, then we'll make the call."

"Yes, I could call some prospective clients right now, but if I learn how to use the latest CRM or webinar tools first, then I can be more efficient. That's what I should do."

Your mind tries to convince you that spending a lot of time on something gives it intrinsic value. It doesn't. Your mind reassures you that hours of work equate with being productive. They don't.

Being productive has nothing to do with how many activities you complete in a given day. It has nothing to do with how much time you spend working on things.

True productivity come from focusing your efforts on creating real value for your business and working directly toward your goals.

The irony is that the activities that are most comfortable are typically things that are nice to have. Yes, it's nice to have a well-designed website, to tweak your social media profiles, to research new technology.

But the activities that are most uncomfortable, like calling a prospective client or writing a new article for a trade publication and promoting it, are the things that will create the greatest value for your business. These are the things that produce tangible results.

BUILD SYNDROME

Over the years, I've written numerous articles on the Consulting Success website about a phenomenon I call the Build Syndrome. It's as relevant today as ever. The Build Syndrome is a highly contagious and debilitating form of procrastination.

It occurs when you spend most of your time working hard on less-than-productive activities. You think, plan, study, tinker, then you think, plan, study, and tinker some more. This creates a routine that becomes comfortable for you, and you get into a rut.

Since it feels like you're doing meaningful work, you fool yourself into thinking that you're being productive. After all, you're spending your time building actual things!

You're creating plans, putting together presentations, webinars, brochures, and business cards, strategizing your funnels. Just look at all the wonderful things you are spending your days designing, building, and creating!

At the same time, however, you rarely leave your office. You spend hours planted right there in your seat, staring at the computer screen, but it feels like you're working so hard. You go home at night mentally exhausted, patting yourself on the back.

The problem is, you're not doing the single most important thing you can do to grow a business. You're not getting in front of your ideal client.

I speak to many consultants who have made all these plans, come up with so many ideas, and created so many perspectives on what might happen at some point in the future. They are fully prepared for breakthrough success and growth. Unfortunately, they aren't doing the one thing that will actually bring about that growth: they aren't having conversations with prospective buyers.

If you're not spending your time having conversations with buyers, you aren't building your business. It's as simple as that. No other work that you do can fill that void.

This was Martin's problem. He spent hours researching relevant topics, thinking and planning and preparing, but he rarely left the building. Nobody was holding him accountable on a daily basis to meet with prospective clients, so it became too easy for him to put it off.

When I began meeting with him, I was able to provide some of the accountability he lacked, and he started going out there and talking to real buyers. Guess what happened? His consulting business took off. In short order, his company started landing six-figure projects.

How did he overcome the uncomfortable?

He did what we all must do. He identified the activities that would accomplish his goals and admitted to himself that these things were difficult for him. Once he did

that, rather than hiding in his office and hoping everything would sort itself out, he took action. Did he suddenly become comfortable getting out there and talking to
prospective buyers? No, but he did it anyway. With a little
encouragement from me, he went for it.

He simply had to act despite his discomfort. He still
faced the unknown, and he still had many concerns. Some
parts of his own marketing plan terrified him. It's not easy
to put yourself out there, to set up meetings, to contact
people, to sell your services, to try to win people over.
Martin knew that, but he had finally realized the key to his
own progress.

What is that key? It is simply this: the only way to get
comfortable doing the uncomfortable is to start doing it.
Start calling those clients and scheduling those meetings.
Start contacting those editors. You'll prove to yourself that
you can do it, and you'll become familiar with it. The more
you do it, the more you'll learn, and the more results you
will produce.

Elon Musk made millions from his internet company
PayPal. He could have retired in comfort and ease, or he
could have invested in something safe. What did he do instead? He did something that many people thought was
foolish. In 2002, he invested most of his PayPal money in
his own space transport company, SpaceX.

He had no experience in the aerospace industry, none whatsoever, but he went for it. He was far outside of his comfort zone, and he probably had many days where he had to choose between doing easy tasks or taking big risks. Clearly, he took the risks, and in 2008, SpaceX won a $1.6 billion contract to resupply the International Space Station. In 2017, the company achieved the first successful launch and landing of a used orbital rocket.

Lucille Ball became one of the most famous television actors in the history of the medium, but most people don't realize the hard road she took to get there. She attended the John Murry Anderson School for the Dramatic Arts in NYC as a teenager, hoping to learn the skills to break into Hollywood. However, the instructors there were less than impressed, and by her own admission, she faced constant criticism in front of her peers.

As she later confessed, "All I learned in drama school was how to be frightened." None of her instructors thought she had a chance, and they actively encouraged her to seek another profession. The school even wrote a letter to her mother at one point, informing her that Lucy was wasting their time.

Despite this uncomfortable experience, and the pain of facing constant criticism, Lucy decided to pursue her career in acting. Through years of struggle, working as an unknown fashion model, a chorus girl, and a low-paid B-movie actress, she endured and kept striving. She knew what she wanted. She had a dream, and she wouldn't let go of it, even though many steps along the way must have been difficult and scary.

Her major success didn't come until she landed her own network sitcom, *I Love Lucy*, and the rest is history. The show became one of the most influential sitcoms of all time, and Lucy went on to win multiple Emmy awards.

What do Elon Musk and Lucille Ball have in common? Not much, except they shared a mindset of success. They both shunned the easy and the comfortable in order to chase bigger dreams. They took the risks, faced the challenges, and they got out there and did what they had to do in order to make their dreams happen.

The choice is in your hands. You can keep filling your days with busy work. You'll stay safe, like a boat docked in the harbor, surrounded by what you already know. Or you can venture out, stare fear right in the face, and sail toward the horizon, despite the risk of rough seas and the unknown. That's how you achieve what you really want in life and in business.

Success doesn't happen when you simply sit and wait for it to happen. If you want it, you have to go after it.

MINDSET REVIEW

- Often, the activities and actions that you feel most uncomfortable doing are the ones that will create the most value and help you to achieve the most progress.

- These become more comfortable and easier to do once you have experience doing them and you start seeing results.

- You won't see results if you don't work at them. Thinking about them, planning what to do, even trying isn't enough. Your commitment to consistent action-taking is a requirement for success.

- It's easy to fill your calendar with tasks and activities that give you a sense of accomplishment, but real progress comes from doing high-value tasks. Identify the core activities that are necessary to reach your goal and focus your time solely on those things.

5

WORRY WELL

Successful people worry, but they worry well.

Kenneth Chenault, the chairman and CEO of American Express, attributes his success in large part to worrying. As the story goes, he makes a list each night before bed of the three things he's most worried about. The next morning, he takes that list and goes to work dealing with those three issues. Instead of avoiding worry altogether, he channels it in a productive way that helps him stay on top of potential problems.

Jeff Bezos of Amazon doesn't worry about failure. He only worries about regret. As he has famously said, "The one thing I might regret is never having tried." That singular worry drives him to keep pushing and taking risks. It eliminates the hindrances that an overly cautious person might have. In other words, it's good for him and good for his company.

One afternoon, during a coaching session with one of my clients, Edward, he said something that struck me. We were sitting in the back corner of a café, discussing his concerns and feelings. Edward was in the middle of a major transition, shifting the focus of his business. He had every reason to be stressed out.

Instead, he told me, "Worry serves me well."

Worry is the constant companion of consultants. I've seen it, and I've experienced it. Consultants worry a lot. With so many uncertainties, so many things to plan, so many decisions to make, it's hard not to worry constantly. It's something I often discuss with clients.

That particular day, as Edward and I talked about his upcoming transition, I encouraged him that worrying is natural and can be a good thing. It's normal to have concerns, and, in fact, it can be beneficial. If you aren't concerned about anything, if you aren't thinking about areas that need improvement, things you could do differently, then you run the risk of becoming complacent.

THE DANGER OF COMPLACENCY

Complacent people aren't progressing. They've accepted the notion that they have everything they need to be successful. Even if that's true, it's always good to look for ways to improve what you're doing. It's always smart to think about how to deal with potential problems before they arise.

Though it might sound like a contradiction, worry is no reason to get stressed out. Believe it or not, it's possible to worry without stressing out. Consider the case of Kenneth Chenault. He's not pacing around his house at night, so sick with worry he can't sleep. Instead of letting the stress get to him, he has come up with a simple system that allows him to channel his worry in a meaningful way. In fact, he's using it to help him take action.

Most entrepreneurs will tell you they worry a lot. They're always thinking about their businesses, considering all angles, planning for all possible scenarios. That's healthy. What makes worry detrimental is when you spend too much time dwelling on the negative, expecting the worst, and sinking into despair.

TAKE TIME TO REFLECT

Find healthy ways to deal with stress. Even small things can get to you, building up over time until you're thoroughly miserable. It's important to create time for quiet reflection. Exercise and meditation, in particular, are great options, so try to work them into your schedule.

Surrounding yourself with the right people is also helpful. By spending time with friends and acquaintances who have already achieved success, you can learn from their example. Observe how they deal with and overcome worry, then you can reflect and gain clarity during your quiet times.

Also, make sure you aren't worrying about the wrong things. A lot of worry is about theoretical outcomes that are ultimately unrealized. For example, you might work furiously on a specific proposal, trying to make it perfect, because you're afraid another opportunity won't come along. Or you might put off meeting with a prospective client because you don't feel ready, and you're worried about making mistakes.

"This is my chance," you might tell yourself. "I can't afford to mess it up. I have to get everything right!"

You're treating the opportunity like it's your last chance, and worrying accordingly, but it isn't. It's never your last chance. There are always more opportunities to meet new clients, to keep learning and growing, so all of that worry is a waste of emotional energy.

If it's not motivating you to take positive action, then it's not helping you. If it's causing you to hold back, to sit in a dark room, tapping your feet and waiting for the worst to happen, then it's not doing you any good. If you're going to worry, worry well.

Worrying well means considering all of your options without becoming so obsessed over them that you can't move forward. It's about recognizing possible risks then continuing to act.

Look at all of the possible paths before you, select the one that best aligns with your business plan, and move in that direction. Focus is the key. If worrying helps you to stay focused on the things that matter, then it's serving you well. And that's the point that Edward came to understand.

As a business owner, you are constantly faced with new opportunities, new ideas, employment offers, and resources. Stay focused on the things that help your business grow. Hone your worry in a healthy direction, so that it constantly spurs you on.

If you do that, then worry will become a constant companion that you learn to appreciate.

MINDSET REVIEW

- It is normal to worry as you enter the unknown. Recognize the feeling, accept it, but don't let it prevent you from going after the result you want.

- Don't become complacent. The market is always moving. You can't stay where you are indefinitely.

- You're either improving or declining. Even if you're at the top of your game, if you don't continue to sharpen your skills and adjust your marketing, your competition will, and eventually they will surpass you.

- Create quiet times of exercise or meditation, so you can reflect on your situation in a healthy way.

- Surround yourself with successful people, so you can see how they have dealt with and overcome many of their worries.

- Make sure you aren't worrying about the wrong things. A lot of worry comes from theoretical outcomes that are ultimately unrealized.

- Hone your worry in a healthy direction, so that it constantly spurs you on. Focus on things that will help grow your business.

6

OUTREACH IMPERFECTED

sensed her hesitation, her face framed in a window at the corner of my computer screen.

I caught glimpses of the office behind her, and I could tell she kept it neat and clean, everything in its place. On a shelf above her right shoulder, she had pictures of various important people she'd met during her career. Degrees, certificates, and awards hung in frames on the wall. Clearly, she'd had an impressive career.

Belle is an expert in her field. She's worked for governments and large global organizations. Many have turned to her for advice, but something was troubling her.

"What is the most important step you could take right now to get more business?" I asked her.

Despite her vast experience, she didn't answer right away. I could see the wheels turning in her head as she tried to come up with an answer. She fidgeted in her seat.

I tried a different approach.

"How do you win new business?" I asked. "What is the first essential thing you must do?"

She ceased fidgeting and sat up straight.

"Oh, that's easy," she replied. "I meet with a prospective client."

"Exactly! If you want to win a new client, you have to meet with a client. So what are you doing right now to get in front of your ideal client? What are you doing to create more conversations with them?"

"The thing is…" She hesitated again, frowning. She started to say something, caught herself, and started over. "The fact of the matter is, Michael, I'm not sure if my message is perfected yet. I'm not ready to get in front of new clients without the right message. Plus, my website really needs to be updated. If I direct prospective clients to the website right now, it might reflect badly on my business. I'm working on it. In a few days, a couple of weeks max, it'll be perfect, and then I can reach out to new people more effectively."

SEEKING CERTAINTY

Most consultants know that getting in front of clients and creating conversations with them is the key to growing their business. Despite this, many of them find reasons to avoid it. As we've seen in previous chapters, there's always an excuse, always some reason to delay, always something else to work on first.

Why do consultants do this?

Because they want certainty. They want a guarantee that what they're doing will work, so they wait for conditions to be as perfect as possible. They continue to work on other things. They keep making excuses.

The website. The blog. More research. More study.

But when someone craves certainty from something they have yet to do, the only result will be ongoing uncertainty. It's only when they take action toward what they want to achieve that they will start to find the certainty they are looking for.

If you've ever tried to squeeze the juice out of an orange, you know that you get most of the juice when you first start squeezing. After a few seconds, you're still squeezing with all your might, but you're only getting a few drops.

Some consultants are still trying to get the last of the juice out of the orange before they take a drink, but at this point, they're only wasting time and energy.

"I need more details, more reports, more videos, more stuff to study, before I take action."

No, if you're thirsty, what you need to do is pick up the glass and take a drink.

What are the most common areas of uncertainty for consultants when it comes to meeting with clients? Message and marketing. Without a message that works well, they will struggle to attract clients, so crafting that message, also known as a value proposition, becomes crucial. However, during the crafting of the message, many questions arise.

Will it resonate with the ideal client?

Will it garner attention and interest?

These questions lead to doubts, which result in an endless tweaking of the message. The only way to find out if your message works is to put it into action.

Maybe you're a perfectionist, and you want to know that everything is in order before you take action. You work hard to position every word, and you wait for the stars to be aligned. The problem is, attaining perfection is extremely rare, and even when it happens, it takes time.

Even the greatest and most successful companies in the world, and their most spectacular products, have imperfections. Think about airlines, cars, luxury goods, world-class service businesses. Can you name a single one that never made a mistake or found an error in their product, service, or offering?

The Coca-Cola Company has been around for a hundred and thirty years. They've grown into one of the largest corporations in the world with one of the most recognizable brands. Nobody would dispute the fact that they've become the most successful soft drink company of all time.

However, they famously faced a rather unusual problem when they first introduced their product into China. Local merchants weren't sure how to translate the name of the company into Mandarin Chinese characters, so many of them simply put together symbols that sounded phonetically similar. Unfortunately, because of the nature of Chinese writing, each of these symbols carried a separate meaning, so even though they might have been pronounced in a way that sounded like "Coca-Cola," they often created bizarre sentences. The most famous examples were "female horse fastened with wax" and "bite the wax tadpole." Do either of those sound like beverages you'd want to consume?

Eventually, the company came up with the closest Mandarin equivalent, "ke kou ke le," which translates as, "to permit the mouth to be able to rejoice." In terms of message, that's much better, but it took time to get there. By then, the soft drink had already been released into the Chinese market and proved popular, even with those strange early translations.

Perhaps the company's most famous mistake happened in 1985, when they attempted to change the formula for the soft drink, declaring it "the new taste of Coca-Cola." The decision came about when nervous executives saw the soft drink losing ground in the market. During blind taste tests, consumers seemed to prefer the sweeter taste of their chief rival Pepsi.

In order to compete, Coca-Cola executives decided to change their famous formula to something a little closer to Pepsi. They introduced this brand-new version of their classic product in April 1985, promoting it as New Coke.

Despite a massive marketing push and initial curiosity from the public, the company faced backlash in some of their biggest markets from people who didn't like the new taste.

In fact, after a relentless wave of angry letters and phone calls, the company soon reintroduced the original formula under the name Coca-Cola Classic. Pepsi was able to play off this failure by boasting in their ads that they'd won the so-called "Cola Wars."

In 1992, the new product was renamed Coke II, but by then, it had mostly become a cautionary tale for marketers. By the end of the millennium, it was completely off the shelves, which is why you can't go down to the nearest grocery store and buy New Coke today.

The failure of New Coke has become one of the most famous marketing blunders in modern corporate history, but what has the long-term impact been on the company? The Coca-Cola Company not only survived that mistake, they learned from it and continued to grow. In fact, they bounced back from the New Coke fiasco relatively quickly, regaining lost ground in the market.

New Coke wasn't the only time the company tried something new and failed. Do you remember OK Soda from 1993, the company's unsuccessful attempt to reach Generation X? It lasted less than two years on store shelves. How about Coca-Cola BlāK, their strange combination of soda and coffee? Introduced in 2006, it was discontinued in 2007.

Part of what has made the company so successful is their willingness to take risks with new products and new marketing. Sometimes, they don't get the result they want, so they learn from the experience and adjust their approach.

If Coca-Cola doesn't have to be perfect in order to become one of the largest companies in the world, why do you? Success requires taking risks, and taking risks means stepping boldly into uncertainty.

Anytime you start something new, or do something you haven't done before, you face uncertainty. This is as true in marketing as it is anywhere else in life. A little bit of fear is normal and healthy, but you mustn't let it hold you back.

When it comes to marketing, there are specific strategies that work well for consultants to grow their businesses. In fact, that's what the Consulting Success Coaching Program is all about. However, the reality is, even when you know exactly what you need to do, you will still feel a degree of uncertainty and fear. When that happens, the best thing you can do is to take action right away. Don't let the fear take root and become an obstacle.

You find out what works when you test it. Put it out there, see what kind of response it garners, and then you'll know whether or not to tweak it.

THE MAGIC BEHIND THE MAGIC

When you fail to take action, when you're not doing outreach because you aren't a hundred percent confident that your message and marketing will hit the mark the first time, you wind up twiddling your thumbs, waiting for ideal clients to somehow find you.

It's a marketing strategy that is built solely on hope. In the end, you're left relying on your network and referrals, but when the referral well dries up, you're in trouble. That's when the real suffering begins.

If you don't do outreach, you'll have fewer opportunities to get in front of your ideal client. That means fewer conversations, fewer proposals, and even fewer projects won. If a door-to-door vacuum cleaner salesman doesn't go door to door, how many vacuum cleaners does he or she sell? If a retail store has nobody at the cash register and nobody on the floor, if they're all hanging out in the break room, tweaking their customer presentations, how many items on the shelves will they sell?

There is no substitute for getting out there and meeting with prospective clients. You just have to get up and start doing it. Once you commit to outreach, a magical thing happens: you start to build momentum. That momentum puts you in front of more and more ideal clients, which means you'll have more conversations and more opportunities to identify value and make proposals to buyers. That leads to more business.

Have you ever met someone who had less education and less subject matter experience than you who was also somehow more successful than you? How can that be?

The answer is simple: they take action.

Your message and your marketing don't have to be perfect to create the results you want. Success doesn't demand complete accuracy right from the start. You can adjust and optimize things along the way.

Successful people recognize when they have something of value to offer. They've created a product or designed a service that they are confident will work. They might not have complete certainty, but they know that the best way to build confidence in their message and marketing is to test it. To put it out there and see what happens.

Implement and take action on it. That's what successful people do.

Coca-Cola put New Coke out there, and it didn't work. But you know what? They've put hundreds of popular products in markets all over the world and launched countless marketing campaigns that have brought in billions of dollars in revenue. The magic behind the magic is learning as you do outreach. When you put your product, your service, or your message out there, you will quickly discover what resonates with your ideal clients and what doesn't.

You take those results and the data from your outreach, and you use it to adjust and optimize. You're building your business and perfecting your message at the same time. As you do that, your outreach becomes consistently more effective, and eventually you get to the point where it feels easy to attract high-value clients.

Turn your doubt into a strength. Push into it. Don't stop taking action. If you don't try, nothing happens. If you try, something spectacular might.

IMPERFECT ACTION
Successful consultants practice Imperfect Action.

They see and relish every opportunity to put something out there, to benefit from the learning process, because they know that adjustments and course corrections are often necessary. The SpaceX program of Elon Musk is built around the idea of reusable rockets. They've had a number of spectacular setbacks along the way, including rockets that exploded on the launch pad, but you know what? They've learned from every setback, and the program continues to get better and better. Their successful landings are truly a sight to behold. What if Elon Musk had said, "No, we can't launch a rocket until we are a hundred percent certain that nothing could possibly go wrong?" He'd never get anything off the ground. Many of the successful products that we know and love are the result of people taking Imperfect Action. The first electric bread toaster was created by an inventor named Alan MacMasters in Scotland in 1893. It had obvious design flaws, chiefly that the heating element, which was made of iron wiring, melted after repeated use.

It wasn't until 1905 that an alloy was created to fix the problem. From there, a more successful version of the toaster was released by General Electric in 1909. Called the D-12, it was still remarkably crude. The toaster still had a long way to go, but companies continued to tweak and improve the design.

It's fair to say that the toaster has been one of the most successful appliances of the modern age, but it was the result of Imperfect Action.

You have a choice. You can either harness the power of Imperfect Action to your advantage, or you can hide behind theoretical perfection and do nothing.

The quickest and most direct path to success, to growing your business, is to reach out to your ideal client with a message that you believe speaks to their needs, problems, or desires.

Don't wait for perfection. Reach out to them now. Make them aware you exist and engage in conversation.

MINDSET REVIEW

- Certainty comes from taking Imperfect Action and seeing with your own eyes what works and what doesn't.

- The more you approach ideal clients, the more you will be able to hone your message and make it more effective at generating a response.

- The only way to improve your marketing is to start marketing and apply what you learn. Test your message, track the results, and make adjustments along the way.

- Even the biggest and most successful brands make mistakes. They learn how to improve by trying and implementing, not merely by thinking and planning.

- You don't need to reinvent the wheel and start from scratch. A coach or mentor can help you reduce your learning curve.

7

OFFERING YOUR EXPERTISE

It was six in the morning, Japan Standard Time, and I'd been awake for an hour. I sat down at my desk, the quiet sounds of the city seeping through the window. My family was asleep, every room still, as I opened Skype on my laptop and gave Mitch a call.

Not the best time to be making a Skype call? Perhaps, but Mitch was on the Pacific Coast in the US, where it was the middle of the afternoon. I'd been in Japan for three months working with a client. When you have clients all over the world, juggling time zones is something you learn to do.

Mitch already had a successful consulting business when he joined our Consulting Success Coaching Program. A former ad agency owner, he'd had great success in the past, but when I called him from Japan for our kick-off call, one thing became clear right away.

His level of expertise as a consultant was impressive, but the value he delivered for his clients didn't align with the results he was getting. He had a newsletter that was read by thousands of prospective clients. They eagerly awaited each new article that he published. So what was going wrong?

"Mitch, how many leads and inquiries do you get each time you send out a newsletter?" I asked.

"Let me think." A long pause. "Very, very few," he said, finally.

"Okay, send me over a copy of your latest newsletter."

He emailed me the latest issue, and when I took a look, the problem became clear right away. Mitch wasn't making a clear offer. He wasn't suggesting a next step to his readers. As a result, few people were taking one. When I pointed this out to him, it was like someone had finally turned on the light. A simple problem with a simple solution was costing his business a lot of money.

A few days later, I spoke to another client, Patrice, who was having a similar problem. The industry that Patrice focused on differed from Mitch's, but it came down to the same issue. She was great at setting up meetings and arranging opportunities to have conversations with clients, but when it came to making a clear offer, she always hesitated.

Mitch and Patrice aren't alone. Many people feel apprehension when it comes to making an offer. They're afraid to sound salesy, afraid the buyer will suddenly dislike them or lose respect for them.

THE BUYING PROCESS

You can't afford to think that way. Making an offer is as integral to growing a business as tires are to a car. Without them, you're not going very far. When you look at the buying process for professional services, the importance of making an offer becomes clear:

Of course, in reality, there might end up being additional steps beyond these five. For example, you might need multiple rounds of follow up with a particular client, or several conversations over the course of multiple meetings. However, what remains true in every situation is how to get from Conversation to Proposal: make an offer. There is no other way.

An airplane doesn't get you from New York to Los Angeles without wings, and you don't get a client from Conversation to Proposal with making an Offer. That doesn't mean you have to be aggressive or back someone into a corner. That's not how you sell professional services.

All you're doing is presenting an offer and suggesting the next step to the buyer. The buyer is having a conversation with you in the first place for a reason. What you have to say is important enough for them to take the time to speak with you. That fact alone means they are interested in what you can do for them.

They have a problem and need a solution, or they have a goal and need to reach it. Either way, they are hoping you can help. Keep that in mind the next time you meet with a prospective client.

Imagine for a moment that the person you're talking to is someone you care deeply about, someone you already have a relationship with. Let's say it's your own mother. She's just told you about a problem she's having with her CRM system. Yes, your mother has a CRM system. Just go with it.

"The data I need to run my business isn't displaying properly," she says. "Someone came in to fix it, but a few days later, the problem started creeping up again."

Your sweet old mother is considering changing CRMs because she feels like she's wasted so much time and effort. Fortunately, you happen to be an expert in CRM and business automation. You were raised right! As your mother tells you about her problems and expresses her frustration, you can already think of a few solutions.

So what do you do? Just sit there and nod your head? When she's done talking, do you say, "Well, Mom, I'm sorry to hear about your CRM problem, but I wish you the best?"

No, of course not. You offer a suggestion, or a resource, or a solution that will resolve the problem. You might even go so far as to say, "I've helped so many people with their CRMs. Why don't I take a look at your setup, so I can suggest a possible solution? Maybe I'll be able to show you a way to run the whole thing more efficiently and effectively, so your business processes will be smoother. Would that help, Mom?"

Of course that's what you'd say to your own mother. What kind of son or daughter would you be if you didn't? And you'd say the same thing to a good friend. When you find out that someone you care about has a problem that you can resolve, you offer to help.

Why is it so hard, then, to make an offer to a client? They are sitting across the table from you, sharing their problems, and you have a product or service that can help. Why do you feel so uncomfortable making the offer?

I see it all the time, consultants who are struggling because they don't make clear offers as part of their sales and marketing activities. They might believe that holding back won't impact their business, but it does. It always does.

After all, if you don't tell your ideal client how you can help them, how will they ever know? Your clients may be smart, but they can't read your mind. If you've identified that you can add value for someone, let them know. If you don't, you are doing them a disservice, and your business loses an opportunity.

It's a loss for both parties.

Take the same scenario and put it in another industry. A man who owns a lawn care business comes to your door. He boldly rings your doorbell, and when you answer, he gives you a big smile and a firm handshake.

You might not enjoy when salesmen come to your door, but this guy is so friendly and so easygoing that you can't resist having a conversation with him. Plus, you see the logo of a lawn care business on the side of his truck, and it just so happens that your yard is a weedy, overgrown mess.

"Do you have trouble keeping it mowed?" he asks. "It looks like it might be a real frustration for you."

"Oh, it is," you confess. "I own an old push lawnmower, and it doesn't have a lot of horsepower. As you can see, my yard has a lot of weeds, especially crab grass, so I always break my back when I try to mow it. Plus, it kicks up my allergies, and I sneeze the rest of the day."

"I sympathize," he says. "That sounds terrible. When is the last time you mowed?"

"It's been well over a month," you reply. "I keep putting it off. I wish there was an easier way."

"I've met many people who hate mowing their yard," he says. "It's a common problem, but your yard might be one of the worst I've ever seen."

He gives you a gentle pat on the shoulder and stares at you awkwardly for a few seconds.

"Well, have a good day," he says, finally.

He shakes your hand again, turns, and leaves. He never tells you about his lawn care services, never shares his prices, and never makes a clear offer. Apparently, he expects you to figure it out on your own and ask him.

As he walks away, his slumped shoulders suggest that he's disappointed. He might even be wondering what he did wrong.

Why didn't that customer ask me to mow his yard? I communicated the need clearly. I don't understand.

What happens? You both lose out. He fails to sell his services, and you're stuck with that weedy, overgrown yard, and all because he didn't make a clear offer at the end of the conversation.

What should the lawn care business owner have said?

"I can understand why you hate mowing your yard. Fortunately, I can take care of it for you. I'll get rid of the weeds, keep the grass trimmed, and you'll never have to worry about it ever again. Does that sound good to you? Great, here's how we can get started."

That's what you needed to hear. Instead, he waffled at the point of making an offer and wound up walking away empty-handed. Can you see how absurd that is? Why do so many consultants do the same thing when it comes to their services? It's a consultant's job to serve clients and provide them value, to help them overcome challenges and get closer to their goals.

There's nothing wrong with feeling uncomfortable making an offer when you're just getting started in your business, but you must realize that if you truly care about the prospective client, you have to share with them how your services can help. It's your responsibility. Suggest a solution and reveal the next step.

That doesn't make you pushy. The buyer can always say no. At least give them the choice. When the offer is clear, purchasing the service becomes a simple process for the buyer. When I shared all of this with Mitch, it helped him shift his mindset. He updated all of his marketing materials and added clear offers in his newsletter. The result? He now receives four times more leads every month, and his business is growing faster than he can handle. That's a great position to be in.

I've observed a similar transformation in many of the clients I've worked with. Once they recognize that the best way to help someone is to make a clear offer of their product or service, their business soars to new heights. In fact, your business will grow in direct proportion to the number of offers you make.

Every piece of marketing copy or communication that you create, every conversation you have with a prospective buyer, is an opportunity to make an offer. As soon as you identify that a next step with a client would be valuable for them, give them a high-level view of what a solution and next step looks like and how it would benefit them. Then, simply ask, "Would that be a good fit?"

No pressure. No strong-arm tactics. No relentless persuasion. Simply make an offer of service, support, and value. What's the worst that could happen?

Where does all the hesitation and fear come from, anyway?

Let's find out.

MINDSET REVIEW

- The most successful consultants and marketers consistently make offers.

- The more offers you make, the more you'll learn what the market wants and doesn't want. That allows you to make improvements, which will result in more sales.

- You can't land a client if you don't make them an offer.

- There's nothing wrong with feeling uncomfortable making an offer when you're just getting started in your business, but if you truly care about a prospective client, you have to share your offer with them. It's your responsibility.

8

WHERE YOUR BELIEFS COME FROM

Rob's father came home from work most nights in a bad mood, shouldering his way through the door and dropping into his favorite chair. He'd flick on the television and watch the news, scowling at the screen.

If Rob asked his father for anything at that time, he was invariably told, "Don't start begging right now, okay? I'm tired. Let your father relax."

If he persisted, he'd get an angry look and a dismissive wave of the hand. "I work hard all day, come home exhausted, and the first thing you do is pester me for stuff. Give it a rest!"

Eventually, Rob learned that if he wanted anything from his father, he had to approach him in a different way. He couldn't make a direct request. Instead, he had to circle around the issue and sneak toward it, trying to catch his father unaware.

To this day, Rob finds it difficult to make a direct offer to a client. Rather than saying, "Here's how I can help you," he holds back or dances around the issue.

His belief that making a direct offer is ineffective comes directly from his upbringing.

EMOTIONAL SUPPORT

So where do your beliefs come from?

Over the last eighteen years of working with consultants, I've found that discovering the origins of a consultant's beliefs can create tremendous clarity for them. Our beliefs are not always the result of conscious choices. Instead, they often develop instinctively as a result of experiences.

How we are raised has a significant impact on how we see and react to the world around us. A study in the journal *Childhood Development* found that the kind of emotional support a child receives in their earliest years has an effect on education, social life, and romantic relationships even decades later. [1]

Parents have the biggest impact, of course, but teachers come a close second. A teacher can either provide support to make children feel smart and competent or they can do

---

1 K. Lee Raby, Glenn I. Roisman, R. Chris Fraley, Jeffry A. Simpson. "The Enduring Predictive Significance of Early Maternal Sensitivity: Social and Academic Competence Through Age 32 Years." *Child Development* Volume 86, Issue 3 (2014): 695–708. Print.

the opposite. As with an abusive parent, the emotional scars caused by a bad teacher can last for many years.

In college, I had a language arts professor who didn't care for the quality of my work. Though I did my best, I could see his frustration mounting over the course of the semester. His criticisms got more severe, and finally, he told me, in blunt and unfriendly terms, that my writing was terrible and that I'd never amount to much.

It was an overreaction, and I probably should have just shrugged it off. But I couldn't. The way I looked at it, the professor was the expert. If he said I was terrible, who was I to disagree? Consequently, his comment stuck with me and made me doubt myself.

Fortunately, I was surrounded by friends and family who believed in me. They provided continual encouragement, and in the end, their influence ultimately won out.

Little did that professor know I'd go on to write over eight hundred articles on the Consulting Success website, have my work featured in prominent trade publications and media around the world, and publish several books.

I CAN'T HAVE THAT

A common mindset block that I hear people express is, "I can't possibly have that," where "that" refers to some big thing that they desire. Maybe it's reaching a million dollars in personal income, having a nicer car, a bigger house, or more prestigious clients. Whatever the case, something has led them to believe they can't have it, that it's too far out of reach. Something in their beliefs has placed a limit on their potential.

If a person believes they aren't good enough, it's usually because that idea has been instilled in them by someone else. Maybe someone of importance along the way misled them to think they don't have what it takes to succeed.

Parents, teachers, friends, coworkers, all of these people can have an impact on how you view every opportunity around you. Their influence can propel you to grab hold of a good opportunity and run with it, or they can cause you to put on the brakes and grind to a halt, filled with self-doubt.

At the same time, some people get into the bad habit of comparing themselves to others.

"I don't have an MBA like all of these other successful people, so how can I possibly make it? I come from a poor neighborhood, while all of these other people had money to start with. What chance do I have?"

They've forgotten all of the stories of successful people who grew up poor and unprivileged. Consider the life of John Paul DeJoria, one of the founders of the highly successful John Paul Mitchell hair care company. He grew up in abject poverty in East Los Angeles, selling newspapers and Christmas cards at the age of nine to make ends meet.

When his single mother couldn't take care of him, he wound up in a foster home.

As a teenager, he joined a notorious local street gang just to survive. Finally, a high school math teacher warned him that if he stayed on the same path, he would never succeed at anything. This provided the incentive to make something out of himself, so he graduated high school and joined the Navy.

Unfortunately, success eluded him for years. After the Navy, he worked as an encyclopedia salesman, a janitor, an insurance salesman, and many other things. Eventually, he entered the world of hair care products, working for Redken, but he was fired over a disagreement about business strategy.

Undeterred, he joined forces with hairdresser Paul Mitchell to create a line of hair care products. When their primary investor backed out, they were forced to start the company with only $700.

It was just enough money to create some shampoo and conditioner samples, which they took from salon to salon, trying to make sales. Eventually, a major distributor agreed to take on their line. The rest is history. John Paul DeJoria is now worth over $3 billion. From humble beginnings and difficult circumstances, he's come a long way.

Oprah Winfrey grew up in poverty on a farm in rural Mississippi. At the age of six, she relocated with her mother to a ghetto in Milwaukee. The neighborhood was overrun with crime, gang activity, and extreme poverty. Starting at age nine, she experienced ongoing sexual abuse at the hands of trusted family friends, and this caused her to begin acting out in negative ways.

Finally, after years of bad behavior, including running away from home, she was sent to live with her father in Nashville. He provided the structure and discipline she'd lacked. He required her to learn five new vocabulary words a day, and she transformed into an excellent student and a great public speaker. Oprah became an honors student in high school, won a full scholarship to Tennessee State University, and went to work for a local radio station.

Her career trajectory eventually led her to television, where she built a media empire. She is worth billions today. She didn't allow her early years, those years of abuse and poverty and negative behavior, to define her life or limit her potential.

Richard Branson, of the Virgin Group, is now the fourth richest man in the UK, but he struggled all the way through school. Dyslexia contributed to bad grades, and he did even worse on standardized tests. He transferred schools at thirteen in an attempt to avoid flunking out, but it was no use. He struggled just as much in the new school, and he finally gave up. At the age of sixteen, he dropped out.

For many people, this would have been the end of the story. The rest of their lives would have been defined by their failed education, but Richard was just getting started. He quickly launched his own youth-oriented magazine and began selling ads. Eventually, he started a mail-order record company, experienced modest success, and grew from there. Now, he's one of the most famous self-made billionaires in the world. The business he founded, Virgin Group, controls more than four hundred companies across a wide range of industries. Clearly, he didn't let those early struggles prevent him from achieving tremendous success. As he has famously said, "Do not be embarrassed by your failures, learn from them and start again."

Are you beginning to see a pattern? Many successful people have faced incredible adversity, but because of their mindset, they used their suffering to propel them to greater and greater accomplishments.

While these examples come from the lives of celebrities, there are plenty of regular people who have achieved success outside of the media limelight. There are over four hundred thousand people in the US alone who earn over a million dollars a year.[2]

---

2 Ashlea Ebeling. "IRS Audited One In Ten $1 Million-Plus Earners In 2015, Correspondence Audits Up By A Third." *Forbes.* https://www.forbes.com/sites/ashleaebel-ing/2016/02/25/irs-audited-one-in-ten-1-million-plus-earners-in-2015-correspondence-audits-up-by-a-third

If these people can rise up and achieve success, so can you. The only one who can really set any limitation on you is yourself. No one else has that power unless you give it to them. You get to make the choices that ultimately set the course of your life.

You might see someone else in the same market as you and think, "That person has more experience than me. Why would a company want to engage me rather than him?" And that question leads you to take less action. That question gives you a reason to be unsuccessful.

Instead of trying to compete with someone based on their strengths and your weaknesses, why not focus on your own strengths instead? Consider what makes you unique and be confident in the value you add to clients. If a potential buyer points out a weakness on your part, don't get defensive.

How does this look in practice?

I had a conversation with a buyer once where they said, "You haven't worked in our industry before."

How did I respond?

"You're right. I haven't work in your industry, and that's exactly why you need me. I'm here to help you with my area of expertise: marketing and attracting high-value clients."

The potential buyer got the point, and I won the project.

It's good to be aware of who else is in the market, but you must recognize that there are far more opportunities than any one person or company can handle. In fact, most markets have more demand than supply, so lean into your strengths and share them with the buyer.

CHOICES

Success is a series of choices that you make.

Richard Branson didn't wake up on his sixth birthday and proclaim, "I'm going to be a billionaire someday," and then carry on with his life like everyone else.

No, once a person opens up their mind to the idea of becoming ultra-successful, at whatever age that happens, they begin to make choices and take actions that move them in that direction. This means they do things others are not willing, prepared, or committed enough to do.

If your dream is to earn higher fees, start by learning how to make that happen, discover how you can shift away from charging by the hour or a daily rate. Move your focus to ROI and value.

Simply knowing how to make it happen isn't enough, however, if you don't actually do anything. In the case of higher fees, you won't actually start earning them until you ask for them. All the research in the world can't make up for a lack of action.

To get there, you must begin putting forward the higher number you want to earn, supporting the idea by providing and communicating greater value for your client. In 1987, Oprah Winfrey was earning $8 million a year for hosting her talk show. By 2010, this had increased to $316 million, the highest salary ever for a talk show host.[3] How did she get to that point? Simple. As the value of the program increased, she began to ask for a higher and higher salary.

Recently, former president Barack Obama commanded a speaking fee of $400,000 from Cantor Fitzgerald. As a senator, he would have earned a fraction of that for the same kind of speech. Tom Cruise earns over $20 million per movie now, but when he starred in *Risky Business* back in 1983, he only made $75,000.[4] In all of these examples, as the perceived value of what the individual had to offer increased, they began to ask for more.

I've worked with hundreds of consultants, and one of my favorite ways to support and teach them is by showing them how to increase their fees. James and Christine, two clients I worked with a few years ago, were consultants in the luxury goods industry. They both had amazing corporate backgrounds, and they'd produced truly impressive results for their clients.

When I met them, however, their fees were shockingly low. With all they'd done for their clients, they hadn't really enjoyed the amount of success they deserved. I questioned them at length, trying to determine the reason for the low fees. As it turned out, they believed their fees should fall in line with what other consultants in their industry charged.

They didn't believe it was fair to ask for more, and they didn't think clients would pay more. It was a mix of wrong beliefs and comparing themselves to others that caused them to work a lot harder and get paid a lot less than they deserved.

Through our coaching sessions, I showed them the real value of what they had to offer and reminded them of the typical results they were producing for clients. As a result, their beliefs changed. They let go of the need to be in line with everyone else and focused instead on their value. When they did that, their fees doubled, and their revenue increased by sixty percent, adding hundreds of thousands of dollars to their business.

Ask yourself these questions:

What do you really want to achieve?

What is preventing you from getting there?

What beliefs do you feel are limiting you?

Where did those limiting beliefs come from?

As soon as you make a choice to start moving toward your goals, your beliefs about your own success will change. Yesterday, you thought you couldn't increase your fees. You feared that large organizations wouldn't hire you if you did. Today, as you begin to take action, making higher fees a reality, you'll find your beliefs starting to shift.

In other words, the truth you had about yourself yesterday will bend in order to align with the new truth that you choose to create. Your actions create momentum that propels you toward the result you want. When you do that, you leave those limiting beliefs behind, and good things begin to happen.

As best-selling author Napoleon Hill once said, "Whatever the mind can conceive and believe, it can achieve."

MINDSET REVIEW

- Discovering the origins of your beliefs can create tremendous clarity for you.

- Our beliefs are not always the result of conscious choices. Instead, they often develop instinctively as a result of experiences.

- How we are raised has a significant impact on how we see and react to the world around us.

- The only person who truly has the power to prevent you from reaching your dreams is YOU.

- The choices you make either create the results you desire or prevent you from achieving them.

- Instead of trying to compete with someone based on their strengths and your weaknesses, focus on your own strengths.

9

FINDING THE BEST MODEL

These days, I see advertisements all over the web, in workshops and seminars, from people claiming to have created the best business model.

"Sell high ticket offers!"

"Set up passive income streams!"

"Jump on webinars, podcasts, Instagram, Pinterest!"

When a consultant is inundated with so many new ideas and business models, it can be quite confusing. Every time they come across yet another innovative idea, they might be tempted to think, "Is this what I'm missing? Is this the business model I need?"

And because advertisers are so good at making their new idea attractive, the consultant starts to get excited. "Yes, I think this is it. This is what I've been looking for. It's working for my competitors, so it must be the secret to success!"

These kinds of offers are tempting, particularly when you see other consultants who have more experience, more knowledge, or more expertise than you. It becomes easy to obsess over something they have that you lack, some vital component or business model.

It's a dangerous habit. The practice of comparing yourself to others can be self-defeating, yet even consultants with tons of experience fall into it.

STOP COMPARING YOURSELF TO OTHERS

"I have twenty-five years of experience in the corporate world," Jody said. She sounded calm, and I could tell she was trying to convey confidence. She sat up straight, hands clasped on the tabletop.

I had just started working with her. Jody was new to consulting, but she'd already built up an impressive amount of experience working with some of the top retailers. Her goal was to ramp up her consulting business quickly. The challenge she faced was effectively marketing and selling her services.

"So you're very good at what you do?" I asked, already knowing the answer.

"Yes, I guess so," she replied. She paused, slumped in her seat, and continued, "Actually, to be honest, Michael, there are a lot of people out there who can do what I do, and many of them have more experience consulting than I do. There are plenty of larger consulting firms. I just don't know how to position myself so that a company would hire me."

"Jody, with your twenty-five years of experience working with top retailers, can you help your ideal client create the result they want?" I asked.

"Yes, definitely," she replied.

"Can you communicate that value to a potential client?"

She adjusted herself in her seat, sitting up straight again. "I believe I can."

"That's great. What do you feel is holding you back?" I asked.

"If a company is forced to choose between a large consulting firm which has been in the consulting business a long time or an independent consultant like me, why would they choose me?"

"Why wouldn't they?" I replied.

Do you see the problem here? When she compared herself to others, it diminished her perception of her own worth. She was too concerned about how she stacked up next to larger consulting firms, but once I removed that from the equation, she felt confident in the value she provided her clients.

Throughout my career, I have routinely won projects over larger consulting firms. How do I do it? As I shared earlier, rather than becoming defensive about my own potential weaknesses, I lean into my strengths.

I avoid the comparisons altogether. Consequently, I don't obsess over what a competitor has that I lack, whether it's their experience in a particular industry, their education, their business model, or anything else. I focus on what I have to offer and the results I deliver for clients.

A MATTER OF PERSPECTIVE

Do you remember kindergarten?

Think back. Remember what it was like gazing up at those towering sixth and seventh graders and thinking, "Wow, these people are huge! They're like giants." Remember how intimidating it felt to walk past them in the hallway?

A few years later, when you reached their age, you realized they weren't actually that big. It was simply a matter of perception. What if, as a kindergartener, you had compared them to high school students or teachers instead of five-year-olds? If you'd done that, you would have realized that they were actually pretty small in the grand scheme of things.

This is the danger of comparing yourself to others. Comparisons are always relative, and most of the time, they only give you another reason to pause when you should be moving full steam ahead.

Social media and smartphones have made it easier than ever to find people to compare yourself to. You've got the whole world in your pocket, so you don't have to look far to find someone with more education than you, someone who is older, wiser, who's written a book, spoken on more stages, or has more money than you.

Unfortunately, seeking out comparisons that reflect negatively on us is often our default behavior. We do it almost out of instinct. "Who's ahead of me? Who's doing better? Who's winning more clients? Who has more education, more experience, more expertise?"

The answer to all of those questions is irrelevant.

Dave Thomas, the founder of Wendy's, never finished high school. He began working at a young age, holding a variety of jobs during his pre-teen years. At fifteen, he took a job at a restaurant in Fort Wayne, Indiana called Hobby House. Unfortunately, his family decided to leave their hometown, and Thomas made the fateful decision not to follow them. To support himself, he dropped out of school and began working full-time at the restaurant.

Despite this lack of education, he managed to learn the restaurant business. After serving as a mess cook in the Army during the Korean War, he returned to work at the Hobby House. Around that time, the restaurant became a Kentucky Fried Chicken franchise after a persistent sales pitch from Colonel Sanders. Thomas was soon sent to take control of a franchise in Columbus, Ohio, which began a long professional relationship with Sanders.

In 1969, Thomas launched his own fast food restaurant chain which he named after his daughter Wendy. By the time he passed away in 2002, his restaurant chain had grown to six thousand locations around the world, and his personal worth had reached $99 million. Not bad for a man who left high school in the tenth grade.

Could his lack of education have served as a hindrance to his career success? Of course, if he'd allowed it to. He might have compared himself to other entrepreneurs with college degrees and felt intimidated.

"I can't compete with these people," he might have said. "Glen Bell, the founder of Taco Bell, at least graduated high school. Heck, Fred DeLuca, founder of Subway, graduated from the University of Bridgeport. Who am I to think I can start my own business and succeed?"

Instead of comparing himself negatively to other people, he just kept working hard and growing his business. If he ever had a moment of doubt about his own experience or training, he didn't allow it to slow him down.

J.K. Rowling first got inspiration for her novel *Harry Potter and the Philosopher's Stone* while sitting on a delayed train ride from Manchester to London. The period of time in which she was writing the book, however, was filled with tragedy. First, her mother passed away, and then her marriage fell apart. She wound up living in Edinburgh, Scotland, a divorced single mother on welfare, chapters of the book in progress stored in a suitcase. She was, by her own admission, as poor as it was possible to be without being homeless.

Despite her humble circumstances, she was bold enough to believe that she might find success with the novel. She wrote the first draft in longhand, often while sitting at tables in local cafés with her sleeping baby beside her. Once she finished the manuscript, she encountered a whole lot of rejection, as one publisher after another turned it down. Rather than comparing herself unfavorably to successful authors and limping away in defeat, Rowling persisted.

Eventually, a small publishing house called Bloomsbury saw potential in the book and offered her a contract. The book went on to win numerous awards and become an international bestseller. It spawned multiple sequels and a blockbuster movie series, and Rowling is now one of the wealthiest women in Britain.

Everyone knows the name Steve Jobs. The man behind the name helped create the first successful personal computer and co-founded Apple. He is considered one of the most influential tech minds of the past century. But he only attended college for six months before dropping out.

He was accepted into the prestigious, but rather expensive, Reed College in Portland, Oregon. Unfortunately, his parents had to dip into savings in order to pay his tuition. This bothered him, and it was a major contributing factor to his decision to drop out.

He went on to work in an industry surrounded by people with advanced degrees. It might have been tempting to feel inferior by comparison.

"I can't run a computer company. Most of the big wigs around here have degrees in engineering or computer science. I can't compete with that. I'll get crushed."

Instead, he helped build Apple into one of the foremost innovators in the world of computers and consumer electronics.

Ingvar Kamprad, founder of IKEA, grew up on a small farm in a tiny Swedish village. Despite this inauspicious beginning, he proved to be business savvy at a young age. At only six years old, he figured out how to buy matches in bulk and sell them to neighbors for a profit. He later expanded his catalog to include things like pencils, ballpoint pens, and Christmas decorations.

He founded IKEA in 1943 at the age of 17 using a cash prize he received from his father for good grades, and he began selling locally-made furniture. From this humble origin, he grew IKEA into one of the largest and most recognized brands on the planet. He is now one of the wealthiest people in the world.

Your success isn't dependent on the things you currently lack, whether that's a degree, experience, or prestige. Success is determined by the choices you make. All of the people I've just mentioned can attest to that fact.

Stop comparing yourself to others and start focusing on your own potential.

FIND YOUR MODEL

That means finding a business model that works for you. Instead of trying to emulate other people or jumping on the newest shiny object, think carefully about the kind of consulting business you're trying to create.

What size do you want your company to be? Do you want to be a solo or independent consultant? Do you want to have a consulting firm with a handful of employees, or do you want a firm that has dozens or hundreds of employees?

What income level do you want to achieve? Are you happy generating a quarter of a million dollars a year, or would you rather reach half a million, a million? Would you like to see revenue of $5 million, $10 million, $50 million?

How you answer these questions will inform the type of business model you need to adopt. Rather than chasing the latest fad ideas, embrace the model, strategy, approach, and tactics that will help you reach your goals. As part of this, consider who your ideal client will be. Some popular business models and tactics might not work to reach your ideal client. For example, you might be trying to reach B2B corporate buyers, but many of the models that are promoted online are designed for entrepreneurs or consumer (B2C) markets.

THE IMPACT YOU MAKE

Give some thought to the amount of impact you want to make with clients. It will determine where you need to focus your efforts. For example, if your goal is to have deep impact with individual clients, then you need to spend most of your time working with them directly. There is no substitute for direct consulting or coaching.

On the other hand, if you're looking to provide high-level guidance, sharing strategies and observations from your experience, then you don't need as much personal interaction with clients. You can spend more time writing books, developing courses or online trainings.

Understand what you're trying to accomplish and focus your efforts accordingly. Greater impact with clients comes from higher levels of direct involvement.

COMPLEX OR SIMPLE

What about complexity? Do you want a business with a lot of moving parts? That will require building more infrastructure, hiring more employees, and creating more systems.

Maybe you're satisfied with a simpler business that only provides one type of product or service. Or maybe you prefer a model that doesn't require working with clients directly; you prefer to be more hands-off. Each of these factors will influence the business model you choose.

I humbly suggest you not jump on a business model simply because it's the latest and greatest thing. Just because someone is effective at marketing their idea online doesn't mean it's right for your business. Always take a step back and think carefully before you start running with a new idea.

THE BEST BUSINESS MODEL FOR YOU

Here's the big secret: there is no right or wrong business model.

Selling $50,000 or $500,000 projects to corporate clients is a great model, but so is offering $2,500 or $5,000 packages. For others, selling a $100 or $500 product can be extremely rewarding and profitable.

There are essentially two ways to think about growing your consulting business: volume and value. The approach that you take will greatly influence the model and strategies you adopt. With a volume-based approach, you charge less per project and work with more clients. With a value-based approach, each project is worth more, so you can reach significant levels of revenue and income with only a few clients per year.

Would you rather work with ten clients a year or a hundred? That will determine which way you go. Bear in mind, if you embrace a volume approach, you will need a lot more infrastructure and resources to support all of those clients.

I generally recommend that consultants embrace a value and ROI focused approach, since it allows you to run your business very lean while providing more value per client, but it's up to you.

There is no right or wrong. Consider carefully which model is best for you, for your business, for your situation, and for your goals. Once you've made decisions about each of those things, you can explore different models to find the right fit.

MINDSET REVIEW

- Just because a model works for someone else doesn't mean it's best for you.

- Focus on what you want from your business and life and then choose the model and mindset that best supports that.

- It's easy to obsess over something other have that you lack, but the practice of comparing yourself to others can be self-defeating. Focus on your own potential.

- Your success isn't dependent on the things you currently lack. Success is determined by the choices you make.

- Greater impact with clients comes from higher levels of direct involvement.

- A value and ROI focused approach allows you to run your business very lean while providing more value per client.

10

SMALLTOWN WHEREVILLE

Location is a concern for many consultants. They move to a new city, or away from a big city, and suddenly they find themselves without a network, lacking the connections they once had. They wonder if they'll have to spend time traveling across the country or around the world to serve clients. They fear that their business might be doomed to flounder in isolation.

For some, traveling around the world to serve clients sounds exciting. Others prefer to stay close to home. After all, they left the corporate world in large part because they wanted to spend more time with their spouse and kids, more time enjoying their community. Maybe they wanted to live in a small town or some quieter, more peaceful place. Is that possible? Can a consultant find success without living in the midst of the hustle and bustle?

In short, your location has little to do with your success. Some people use their location as a way to excuse their lack of success. It's easier to blame something external— a new environment, a new city, a lack of relationships or resources that you might have had in your previous job— rather than take responsibility for the situation.

Instead of casting blame or making excuses, I encourage people to accept their current situation and look for the positives. No matter where you're located, you will find opportunity all around you, if you're willing to look for it.

THE MIDDLE OF NOWHERE

I have a client named Elliot who lives in a small town of fourteen thousand way up in Northern California. The majority of his clients aren't located anywhere near him. In some cases, they are in countries far, far away. But for Elliot, location doesn't matter. He works with them virtually, through the internet and over the phone, and it hasn't hindered his success. He's making it work for himself and for his clients.

Another client of mine, Christie, lives in a town of eighty thousand in the middle of Indiana. She left the corporate world because she wanted to spend more time with her five children. Now, she works with organizations all over the world, and she earns more than her corporate salary working fewer hours. Her location is irrelevant.

For both of these clients, their somewhat isolated locations could have been a concern when they first started their consulting businesses. They could've made excuses for why their success would be inhibited.

"I'm in this tiny little Northern California town," Elliot might have said. "I'm at a huge disadvantage because I don't have easy access to potential clients. I'll never be as successful as the big city consultants."

Instead of complaining, both of them found success within a relatively short period of time, and they continue to grow to this day. Through virtual connections, they are finding opportunity around them all the time. Thanks to technology and increasing access to the internet, location has less bearing on a company's success than ever before. You can live practically anywhere and still grow your business.

Elliot and Christie and other consultants like them have one thing in common. They each decided what success looked like to them, and they went out and made it happen. They didn't let location or any other factor hinder or discourage them.

If you decide that your location is a hindrance, your attitude might very well make it so. However, if you focus on what you have and cast aside all of the things that could potentially hold you back, you'll speed past every obstacle and find yourself making progress before you know it.

Sam Walton started his Wal-Mart empire in 1962 with a single discount store in a tiny town in the northwest corner of Arkansas. Would anybody in the beginning have predicted the worldwide success he would achieve with such a modest starting place? At the time, he had no interstate highways nearby and no major cities closer than a few hours away. The population of the town was less than six thousand.

His location could've been a real problem, if he'd let it. Instead, he kept plugging away, working through every setback and challenge, finding ways to grow. It didn't take long for Wal-Mart to experience success. Now, that same company, which he's passed along to his heirs, is one of the largest multinational retail corporations in the world, with thousands of stores in dozens of countries.

Jeff Bezos started Amazon in his garage in Bellevue, Washington. Today, Amazon is the largest online retailer in the world. The first Harley Davidson factory was located in a tiny wooden shed in Milwaukee. The Walt Disney Company began as an animation house located in a one-car garage behind Walt Disney's uncle's house. The Walt Disney Company is now the world's second-largest media conglomerate.

Plenty of successful businesses have started life in modest or out-of-the-way places. What they all have in common is that their founders didn't allow their locations to dictate their growth potential.

Don't worry about where your business is located. If it's a tiny town in the middle of nowhere, a bustling metropolis full of noise and activity, or a lush tropical island, you can make it work for you.

As Elliot once said, "Live where you want to live, instead of where you have to live."

Choosing a place to live is a personal decision, and money is only one consideration. But wherever you wind up, focus on the opportunities you have access to. Chances are you have more opportunities at your fingertips than you've yet realized. Go after them with everything you've got, and you will achieve your goals.

MINDSET REVIEW

- Your location has little to do with your success. No matter where you're located, you will find opportunity all around you, if you're willing to look for it.

- Thanks to technology and increasing access to the internet, location has less bearing on a company's success than ever before.

- Plenty of successful businesses have started life in modest or out-of-the-way places.

11

YOU'RE TOO OLD & TOO YOUNG

irst, there was Bill. He'd ended a decades-long career in order to start his own consulting business. He brought an impressive amount of experience to the table, but he was approaching his seventieth birthday.

"Success is a game for the young," Bill said, leaning back in the big leather chair behind his desk.

The shelves in his office were littered with trophies from all the years he'd spent in the corporate world. His suit and hair were immaculate, and he carried himself like a man who had shouldered great responsibility.

Despite this, he had a weary look on his face.

"It's not too late to achieve real success in your consulting business," I said. "There's nothing holding you back."

"Have you seen my competition?" he said. "They're all young, fresh-faced, and raring to go. I don't have half the energy they've got. I can't compete. No business is going to hire some tired old man over a young, excited consultant."

Then there was Claire. In her mid-twenties, she'd only spent a few years in the corporate world, but her education and training more than made up for it. Still, she had a lot of self-doubt, and it showed.

"I think I'm too young to achieve any real success," she said. "I don't have the experience of the older consultants."

"Can you offer value to your clients?" I asked.

"I think so," she replied. "But no company is going to choose me over someone with twenty or thirty years in the industry. I can't compete. Until I'm a lot older, I'm just going to struggle."

What both of these clients had in common was a belief that age determines success. It cuts both ways—too young or too old—but there's no truth to it.

As you get older, you do accumulate more experience, but experience alone doesn't create success. When I was in my early twenties, I was consulting for billion-dollar companies like Panasonic, Omron, Royal Bank, and the Financial Times.

THE GRASS IS GREENER SYNDROME

You've heard the saying, "The grass is always greener on the other side," but did you know there's an actual Grass is Greener Syndrome in psychiatry?[5] At the root of this syndrome is the idea that something could be better, an idea that becomes so pervasive that it causes the sufferer to obsessively compare themselves with others, robbing them of a sense of stability, security, and satisfaction.

"I should be older. I should have more experience. Then I'd be successful."

"I should be younger. I should have more of that youthful energy. Then I'd be successful."

Someone out there has something you don't have. Someone out there is in a better situation than you are. Beliefs like these prevent people from completely committing to their highest ability.

"I'll never get what I want because I don't have everything I need."

There's a tremendous amount of projection involved in this. You see another consultant with different circumstances than you and assume they must be happier. This leads to ultimate dissatisfaction and might even cause you to run away from your current situation.

---

5 Nathan Felies, MSW, LMSW. "The 'Grass Is Greener' Syndrome." *Relationships in Balance.* https://blogs.psychcentral.com/relationships-balance/2013/03/16/the-grass-is-greener-syndrome/

That's why a young consultant will start to think they're too young and too inexperienced to succeed. They'll begin comparing themselves to consultants who are older, who have years of experience, more money, or better education.

"I can't compete with these people. Nobody's going to choose me over them."

That's also why an older consultant will look at a young, fresh-faced consultant and feel discouraged. They see all that energy, ambition, and speed, and they think, "I can't keep up with these young people. They're going to steamroll me. I'm too old and tired. Sadly, I think I started my consulting business too late in life."

This kind of thinking is self-defeating. Success comes at any age, and the business world is rife with examples.

Jonathan Koon, the son of immigrants from Hong Kong, was only sixteen years old when he launched his auto parts business, Extreme Performance Motorsports. Do you suppose he ever looked at other auto parts companies run by older men and women and thought, *How can I possibly succeed at this? Look at all the experience these other people have. I'm just a teenager. Nobody's going to buy from me.*

If he ever felt a moment of Grass is Greener Syndrome, he certainly never let it slow him down. He hit the big times when he landed MTV as a client, supplying auto parts for their reality shows. He is now worth around $40 million, and he's well on his way to his first billion.

Mark Zuckerberg of Facebook was a billionaire by age twenty-three. In fact, he became wealthy when he was still in college. Did he ever look at competing social media platforms like Myspace and think, *I'm only a college student, so I can't compete with these other sites?* Some might have felt so intimidated that they held back or abandoned their new business altogether. Instead, Facebook overtook Myspace within a few years of launch, and Zuckerberg became one of the wealthiest people in the world.

There are so many examples of young people finding success. Matthew Mullenweg launched the popular web-creation tool WordPress when he was only nineteen years old. By twenty-six, he was worth $250 million. At the age of 8, Abbey Fleck invented a microwaveable bacon cooking plate. Three years later, she acquired a patent for the product, and it became a runaway success, a staple of late-night infomercials. Her product, Makin' Bacon, made her a millionaire.

On the flip side, there are endless examples of people who only found success late in life, after years of struggle and hard work.

Vera Wang is one of the most famous and successful fashion designers in the world. She has designed wedding dresses for celebrities like Sarah Michelle Gellar and Alicia

Keys. Her elegant dresses routinely appear on red carpets. She even designed costumes for the US Figure Skating team at the 1994 Olympics. When she first launched her own company, she was forty years old and had already spent years working for other people.

Celebrity chef Julia Child found success at age fifty with the publication of her first cookbook, *Mastering the Art of French Cooking*. From there, thanks to positive reception of the book, she was offered a cooking show on PBS. In time, she became the most famous celebrity chef in the world.

Arguably the most famous example is Harland Sanders, who toiled away in dozens of jobs throughout his life. He spent time as a farmer, streetcar conductor, lawyer, and an insurance salesman. He failed at most of these jobs. His entry into the food business began when he started selling fried chicken to hungry travelers out of his gas station.

Later, he opened his own restaurant, where his food, particularly his fried chicken, received rave reviews, even earning him the honorary title of "Colonel" from the governor of Kentucky. Sadly, he closed the restaurant at a loss in 1956 when a new interstate highway bypassed the location. He was sixty-five years old, living off Social Security, and still looking for success.

Finally, Sanders hit upon the idea of franchising his chicken recipe. He knew he had a great product, and despite all of his struggles over the years, he was still convinced he could make something out of it. At an age when most people are entering retirement, he began traveling across the country, pitching his recipe to restaurants in city after city. By 1964, there were more than six hundred franchised outlets selling his Kentucky Fried Chicken, and Harland Sanders was a millionaire.

Ray Kroc was in his fifties, struggling to make ends meet as a milkshake machine salesman, when he hit upon the idea of franchising McDonald's, transforming a single hamburger stand in San Bernardino, California into a global fast food chain. Regardless of your opinion about some of the tactics Ray employed in creating his fast food empire, he did achieve an impressive amount of success late in life. John Pemberton, a civil war veteran, was also in his fifties when he launched Coca-Cola, his "delicious, refreshing, and invigorating" soda.

What do all of these examples prove? That age is just a number. Yes, each stage of life offers unique challenges, so age is not completely irrelevant. However, your age doesn't dictate your level of success. You do! You can build a growing, thriving business at sixteen, forty-six, or seventy-six.

MINDSET REVIEW

- You are never too young or too old to achieve the success you desire.

- Although you accumulate experience with age, and experience is beneficial, you can still provide value to clients even when you're young.

- Some people achieve success late in life. Don't worry that you're too old or that it's too late to start your consulting business.

12

THE POWER OF SAYING NO

The results you're getting in your consulting business are largely a consequence of your current way of thinking. That can be hard for some people to accept. It's always so much easier to find external factors to blame.

"No, I'm just having a run of bad luck. There have been some real challenges that have hindered my progress."

I hear those kinds of excuses often, but when I dig into what's happening in a client's business, invariably the biggest piece of the puzzle is always their mindset. For any significant change to occur, you must develop a better way of thinking.

Bjorn was one of my busiest clients, jetting from city to city, running from gate to gate. He was always harried, always in a hurry, with meetings following meetings. He knew all the major international airports like the back of his hand, though he sometimes forgot what city he was in. They all kind of ran together after a while.

Have you ever seen some guy in a nice suit dashing through an airport, sweat running down his face, tie flying over his shoulder, as he hurries to another destination like the end of the world is imminent? That was Bjorn.

He was more than willing to say yes to every opportunity that came his way. As a result, he had a packed schedule all the time, and he traveled non-stop. He only saw his wife a few days out of each month.

He was making a great living, but he wasn't enjoying the lifestyle that he'd always dreamed of. In fact, he was stressed out and afraid to slow down for even a minute. He would frequently spend days traveling to a city, finally arrive at his destination, spend an afternoon with a client, and then get right back on a plane that same evening.

When he made it home, he was always exhausted, too tired to unpack his bags, knowing that in a couple of days he would be right back up in the air. He practically lived at airports around the world. Bjorn was not having fun. Despite the income, he wasn't enjoying his life. He got into that situation because he was afraid to turn down opportunities. He had a big, kind heart, and he was concerned for his clients. He just couldn't bring himself to say no to anyone.

On top of that, he was terrified of disappointing potential buyers. He was a gentle person, and he didn't like seeing the look of disappointment on people's faces.

"What if I say no, and the client gets upset with me?"

"If I spread out my schedule and raise my fees to make up the difference, will clients stop liking me? Will I lose out on future opportunities?"

Do you see how all of this stress was produced by his mindset? His crazy, restless schedule, which was making him miserable, came directly out his fears, anxieties, and thoughts. Bjorn had a scarcity mindset, where he worried, both consciously and unconsciously, that there weren't enough opportunities to go around.

"If I say no to an opportunity, there won't be a next one. I have to accept everything that is placed in front of me."

THE MINDSET OF ABUNDANCE

The most successful people have a mindset of abundance. If an opportunity presents itself and it's not a good fit, they feel free to say no because they are convinced that a better opportunity is right around the corner.

Don't make decisions about taking on a client based on what has happened to you historically. Mentally place yourself where you want to be in your new business model and make decisions that will move you closer to it.

In Bjorn's case, the model he was using was one that worked well for him in the beginning, but in order to get to the next level, to reach the income and lifestyle he wanted, that model no longer served him. He had reached the limit of what it could support, but his scarcity mindset, his fear about what might happen if he turned down some clients and raised his fees, made him reluctant to change anything. At a certain point, you simply have to take the leap in order to change your business model and mindset.

To put it bluntly, avoid taking on low-paying clients and lower-value projects. They are dangerous for your business. You might be tempted to take on such a client because of compassion for that person, or because it will add some revenue, however small, to the business. After all, you might think, isn't making a little bit of money better than making none?

In the beginning, when your business is just starting out, this might make sense. You have to start somewhere, laying a foundation and building a reputation, but that's short-term thinking. Don't make it a habit. The more time you spend with low-paying clients, earning less than you deserve and saying yes to all the wrong opportunities, the more time you're taking away from higher-value clients and projects.

Short-term thinking tells you that any revenue is good revenue, but it's simply not true. If you spend ten hours a week with a less-than-ideal client in a low-paying opportunity, that is ten hours a week, 40 hours a month, you're not spending on attracting a more valuable client and greater opportunity.

"But I need the cash right now, even if it doesn't pay much."

Yes, that makes short-term sense, but if you want to create a sustainable and thriving business, you must shift your mindset, and the sooner you do that, the better. Start focusing on attracting high-value, high-paying clients.

I turned things around for one of my clients, Corrie, simply by helping her improve her value proposition, so she could go after high-value clients. She narrowed her industry focus, learned about the unique challenges potential clients in that industry faced, and created a message that emphasized her experience in providing viable solutions. The end result?

"This has helped me land three hundred percent more clients and increase my revenue four hundred percent."

Quit chasing low-value projects. Strive for those lucrative opportunities.

SPEND TIME WISELY

Take stock of how you're spending your time. Are you making the most of it, or are the hours of your day filled with low-value work? Too often I hear clients say, "I don't have enough time for everything. I can't even spend time with family and friends. I'm so busy. I'm spread so thin across so many client engagements."

Once I get them to take a deeper look at how they're spending their time, they almost always find that they could accomplish more in less time. All they need to do is tweak their schedule and refocus what they're working on. If you must, wake up a little earlier or go to bed a little later. Keep a calendar and commit to it.

Ironically, many of the consultants who have no time for family and friends still manage to watch two or three hours of news or television programs a night. When you're struggling to grow, you might have to cut back on these kinds of activities. Spend that time creating content, focusing on marketing, or writing a book.

Once you've achieved a higher level of success, when you're pulling in those high-paying projects, you'll create greater flexibility and choice on how to spend your time. But for now, prioritize and spend your time on the highest value activities that will grow your business.

TRUE FOCUS

Why do some consultants achieve more than others? Why are they always creating new things, drawing in new clients, leading new workshops? Focus.

Successful people work on improving themselves. They focus their time on projects that lead to growth, and they don't make excuses. We all have the same number of hours in the day, so nobody has an advantage when it comes to time. We simply make choices in how we spend it.

Spend your time wisely. Do you really need to watch that television show right now? Won't there be more time for it when you've reached a higher level of success?

You won't regret cutting things like that out of your schedule. Take the action that's going to create the results you want. Even when it comes to social interactions, you must prioritize. If a friend invites you out for drinks one night, consider whether or not you're going to regret it the next day.

You have to make some sacrifices while you're growing your business. That is inevitable. Friends might occasionally be disappointed. You might not be as sociable as you used to be, or want to be, for a certain period of time. But do you want to achieve the life of your dreams, do you want to get to that next level? If you do, then you must commit to doing what it takes to move in that direction.

My willingness to optimize my time and focus on high-value projects is a big reason why I became a millionaire at age thirty-two. Making sacrifices in the early years of my consulting business enabled me to focus on high-value clients and created a fast-track to incredible success. It's well worth it.

Having said that, let me stress that leisure activities are not meaningless. Once you start experiencing more success, you'll probably get a lot busier. When that happens, you might be tempted to avoid taking time for yourself. Going for walks, spending time with family and friends, taking vacations, and seeking counsel from mentors are all important, and they can contribute to your well-being.

Too many people forget why they sought success in the first place. They become too focused on making money with no clear purpose. If you do that, you will regret it later in life. Always make time for yourself, especially as you become more successful, so you can recharge, reenergize, and avoid burnout.

TRYING TOO HARD TO PLEASE

Some consultants try too hard to please clients. This becomes a problem when you fail to set proper boundaries. For example, a client might ask you to do something that is not part of the initial agreement. If you allow it, that's called Scope Creep.

An unhealthy mindset says, "Hey, you're a good person, a compassionate person, so why don't you go ahead and help this client, even if it's something you didn't get paid to do? They're already paying you well. No need to ask for more money."

The moment you allow a buyer to add work that is not part of the original agreement, you are opening Pandora's box. You are teaching them that it's okay to keep crossing that line. If you allow it once, they'll expect you to allow it again.

It's like setting boundaries for your children. If you let your kids eat candy at midnight one time, there's a good chance that they'll want to do it again. In fact, they'll use it as leverage against you.

"Hey, why can't we eat candy at midnight every night? You let us do it that one time!"

You must set clear boundaries and expectations with your clients. Otherwise, they will take up more of your time and effort than you can afford to give.

If you've already allowed Scope Creep to happen, you must address it as soon as possible. The longer it goes on, the more serious the problem will become. If you wait to address it, the client is going to be far more surprised than they should be.

"You've let it go on so long," the client will say. "Why are you addressing this now? I assumed there was nothing wrong with it."

It benefits both you and the client to set the rules of engagement from the beginning and stick with them. Make the boundaries clear, so if the client asks you to do some extra work outside of the agreement, you can respond accordingly.

"I'd be happy to work with you on that," you can say. "Let me send over a quick proposal of what that extra work would look like, what it would cost, and how much longer it would take."

If there's any objection on their end, refer back to the original agreement that you made and remind them that the extra work is not what you agreed to. Also, point out that any extra work will potentially take away from what you've already committed to do.

That allows the client to reevaluate and determine if it's worthwhile. And if it is, they might say something like, "Okay, let's move forward with this. I'll pay the extra fees, and you can start working on it right after you complete the current project."

If you're doing a good job, buyers will see how competent you are, so it will be easy for them to ask for help on other things. In most cases, they aren't trying to cause problems. They simply have other work that needs to be done, and they are impressed with your capabilities.

But if you accept more work without more compensation, you'll wind up diluting your value and training your client that you're happy to essentially do work for free. Your priority must be the work that you've agreed to and that you're getting paid for.

DISAGREEING WITH CLIENTS

Disagreeing with a client is okay, whatever the issue might be. So often, consultants are afraid that if they disagree with a client, they will upset them and hurt their business.

The reality is that your clients are surrounded by people who say yes to them all the time. They brought you on as an expert because they value your expertise and believe you can help them. As part of that, they expect you to sometimes disagree with them.

Don't allow a mindset of worry to force you to go along with things that you know aren't right.

"The client will think less of me. The client might fire me."

They hired you to speak your mind, to share advice and opinions. If you don't speak openly and honestly, you are doing them a disservice. If you truly want to serve your clients and provide value to them, don't be afraid to speak the truth, even if it means disagreeing with them.

Of course, how you handle this matters. Don't go into a meeting with a client and throw around a bunch of wild, half-baked ideas, and don't be quick to tell them they're wrong. If a client has an idea that you know, based on your experience and expertise, is not going to help them, let them know and share alternatives.

Yes, some people get upset when you disagree with them. Egos can be bruised, but if they are your ideal client, they will know deep down that you are trying to help. They will appreciate your willingness to share your experience and expertise.

Some leaders, when they are surrounded by yes-men and yes-women, find it refreshing when a consultant is honest with them and speaks the truth. That's a role you get to play, and it adds significant value.

DON'T TAKE IT PERSONALLY

What happens when a client says no? What happens when they don't want to move forward with a particular project? Often, the consultant takes it personally. They failed, and now they feel lost, and they want to run away. They decide to throw in the towel on that client and go look for another opportunity elsewhere.

Don't do it. If you give up too early, if you don't re-engage with the opportunity that is right in front of you, you leave a lot of potential revenue on the table. Instead of taking rejection personally and running away, reach out to the buyer.

When you receive an email that says, "We've decided not to move forward," or "We've thought this through, and it doesn't feel like the right time," don't respond with, "I'm sorry to hear that. Goodbye." Instead, try to have another conversation with them. Find out the reasons behind the rejection. Don't do it by email. Pick up the phone.

You'll be surprised at what you find out. Often, a client's first reaction is to reject the project or express reservations about moving forward. That doesn't mean you can't still serve them in some way or provide value. It just requires a little more conversation to figure it out.

Identify what's holding them back or why they don't feel like you're a good fit. Find out why they are hesitant to invest in your services. Support them and discover if there is another way you can serve them. Maybe what you initially proposed isn't what they need. Maybe it's not the right time, in which case you can nurture the relationship, continue providing them with value to stay top of mind, and pick up the conversation a few weeks or months down the road.

If you don't reengage, if you don't have the courage to pick up the phone after the rejection and ask a few questions, then, in all honesty, you didn't really care about that client and winning the project to begin with.

"They're right. It's not a good fit. I don't want to be pushy."

Those are excuses. If you care about the client then you owe it to them and to your business to pick up the phone and reengage. Ask questions, find out what's going on, and see if there's some adjustment or clarification that can be made. You'll be surprised at how many times it works out and turns into a successful project.

WHAT IF THEY DON'T RESPOND?

Sometimes, instead of rejecting your offer, the client just doesn't respond. Some consultants do a lot of outreach, engaging people and trying to create opportunities to meet with their ideal client, increasing visibility in the marketplace, but then they give up on prospective clients too quickly. They might try to contact an ideal client once or twice, maybe three times if they're especially persistent. If they don't get a response by then, or if the response isn't favorable enough, they conclude that it isn't working.

This is part of the short-term mindset. In this day and age, it's hard to blame people for giving up early. So many things are instantaneous. Think about how many things you can access within seconds through the internet and your smartphone: breaking news, maps and navigation, music videos, the weather. Almost anything you want is right at your fingertips.

But marketing and creating clients doesn't happen instantaneously because it requires building relationships. You have to pursue clients with a long-term mindset. If you give up after one, two, or three outreaches, you're leaving opportunity on the table.

According to several studies, it takes an average of seven touch points before an ideal client becomes a paying client. Let that sink in. Three is not enough, neither is four or five or six. In some cases, it might take more than seven interactions. One client read our consulting newsletter for three years before becoming a client. We've been working with him for over two years now.

You must look at it as a process, not a momentary event. Processes take time. Also, buyers go through buying cycles, so people might not be ready to buy a service at the time you first reach out to them.

While you're doing outreach and building a pipeline of opportunities and business, you're helping them to identify problems and understand the value you offer. They start to get a vision for the improvements they could make, and then they begin to consider it. By the time they reach the right point in their buying cycle, when they are actually ready to buy, their decision to work with you is clear.

Rarely will you meet an executive buyer who is ready to buy from you right away. Even if you know a buyer is at a place where they aren't ready to buy, don't discount them, start building that relationship.

Of course, if you have a choice between two potential clients, always go with the one who is ready to buy right away, but don't neglect those who might become buyers down the road. You can still send them meaningful content, keep in touch, and do follow-up.

YOUR FEES ARE TOO HIGH

How do you respond when a buyer tells you your fees are too high? Many consultants have the belief that if a buyer says their fees are too high, it proves that the buyer doesn't value their contribution, or that, in fact, their fees really are too high. In turn, they often reduce their fees. This is the wrong move to make.

It's rarely about your fee. Most of the time, the complaint comes from the client failing to see the true value of what you have to offer. That's your fault, not theirs. You haven't taken the time to clearly communicate the value of your services. First, you have to be willing to see the full value yourself, then you can communicate it to your clients.

Once you've done that, it's time to ask the client some deep and meaningful questions. What are their goals? What are their challenges? Why should they make changes now? What will happen if they don't? What changes can you help bring about? What additional value and benefits will solving their problem provide? What will the end result be?

Questions like these will help you get to the core of what's really important to the client. From there, you can help them see the real value of what you have to offer and how it meets that need. Once you do that, once they understand what the ROI will be, it becomes an easier decision to make.

Suppose someone said to you, "Invest one dollar with me, and I'll give you back ten dollars." If you believed the risk was low and if you trusted them, you would almost certainly take them up on the offer. Why? Because it makes sense, and there's clear ROI.

It's the same situation when you're with a buyer. If you communicate your value effectively, they should be able to see a potential ROI of five to ten times their investment in you. Through the conversation, by asking the right questions, you're helping them to justify the investment in your services. When you do that, you're more likely to get a positive decision in a shorter period of time.

If you're getting a lot of rejections, don't rush to lower your fees, don't take it personally, and don't give up on the buyer. That's what it boils down to. If you've built the relationship, reengaged, helped them to see the real value, and they still aren't interested, then they might not be your ideal client at the moment. Spend time and focus on others for a while.

One key area that I support our clients in is helping them to restructure their sales conversations. Barb is a consultant who works in the healthcare industry. She came to me because she wasn't seeing the results she'd hoped for. When I spoke with her, I quickly realized she was struggling to win over clients.

I showed her how to effectively lead conversations, to delve into a prospective client's real needs and help them see the real value of her services. The results have been dramatic. She's winning more clients, and she's making much more money with each project. As she put it, "I feel like I have more momentum in my business and marketing than I've had in a long time. I've increased my fees by seven hundred percent."

MINDSET REVIEW

- The results you're getting in your consulting business are largely a consequence of your current way of thinking.

- Successful people have a mindset of abundance, not scarcity. They feel free to turn down an opportunity if it's not a good fit because they know that a better opportunity is around the corner.

- Avoid taking on low-paying clients and lower-value projects. If you want your business to thrive, focus on high-value activities and attracting high-value, high-paying clients.

- Spend your time wisely. Prioritize the activities that will grow your business. You might have to make some sacrifices in regard to leisure activities.

- The best way to avoid Scope Creep with clients is to ensure you don't allow it to occur early on.

- It's okay to disagree with a client. Never go along with things that you know aren't right.

- If a client says no to an offer, don't take it personally and don't give up on them too early. Reengage and see if communicating greater value can get things back on track or if there's some adjustment or clarification that can be made.

- Marketing and creating clients requires building relationships. You need a long-term mindset.

- If a client tells you your fees are too high, it means you haven't clearly communicated the value of your services.

13

SUPERMAN & SUPERWOMAN

For the second time in a month, Ronald had rescheduled our meeting. I got a phone call the night before.

"I'm sorry, Michael. I'm way busier than I thought I would be. Can we move our meeting to sometime next week?"

Fortunately, clients rarely reschedule, and since it was only Ronald's second time to do so, I cut him some slack.

"That's no problem, Ronald. Is everything okay?"

"It's fine," he replied. "I just have to get this PowerPoint presentation finished before the end of the week, and it's taking a lot longer than I expected. I've got a lot of images to upload and format. I'm giving a presentation on Monday."

Whether it was a PowerPoint presentation, a spreadsheet, an invoice, or some other low-value work, Ronald often struggled to get everything done while still meeting with clients and coaches, and, as a result, his schedule was jam-packed, and he was always exhausted.

DOING TOO MUCH

Another mindset that hinders progress for consultants is the belief that they can do everything by themselves. It seems like the most affordable option, so they wait as long as possible to hire more people or bring in additional resources to help them grow their business.

I felt this way in the early days of my consulting business. I kept putting off hiring more staff, telling myself I would do it when I had more revenue coming in, or when I landed the next big client. But every time I landed another big client and my revenue increased, I just made the same excuse and put it off again.

Let's explore how additional resources or employees could benefit your business. We're not necessarily talking about building a staff of full-time employees. They could be contractors or even outsourced services. How might they help your business grow?

It's simple. By adding more people, you can assign low-value tasks to others. This frees you up to concentrate on the things that you're really passionate about and create the most value for your business.

What constitutes a low-value task? Any task or activity that someone else could do for you with minimal investment on your part. If you could make more money by spending time doing something else for your business then it's a low-value task. Examples include formatting documents, putting graphics into presentations, adjusting spreadsheets, updating text or images on your website, uploading blog posts, going to the post office, and bookkeeping.

The danger of these kinds of low-value tasks is that you don't always realize how much time they are taking up. You start fiddling with the website, and before you know it, the whole day has gone by. When you add up all the time these low-value tasks consume in the course of a month, you might be surprised. Add them all up over a year and you'd be shocked.

Let's suppose you spend just one hour a day on low-value tasks. That doesn't seem too bad, but over the course of a month, that adds up to about twenty hours. Let's suppose you could get someone else to do all that work for $20 an hour. That's means it would cost you $400 a month to free yourself of all that low-value work.

Many consultants look at that number and think, "Wow, that's $400 I could keep in my pocket. I don't want to spend that."

Not only is it a reasonable expense, but it's actually quite cheap. I'll show you how.

Let's say you want to hire even more experienced people. Suppose you hire someone for $50 an hour to do the low-value work for you. For that much, you could get some incredibly talented people. At twenty hours a month, that adds up to $1,000.

"I can't spend $1,000 a month for someone to update my website and do bookkeeping," you might say. "That money should go into my bank account. Let me wait until my revenue grows. One more client, and then perhaps I can justify the expense."

That mindset is hurting you. If you're spending twenty hours a month on low-value tasks, you are preventing yourself from doing high-value tasks. Instead of working on a spreadsheet, you could be negotiating another deal with a client, creating a proposal, working on your marketing, giving a keynote speech, or writing a book. All of those things have the potential to add significant value to your business.

What would happen if you spent another twenty hours a month dedicated to landing new clients? Let's look at the potential math. Over the course of three months, you've spent sixty hours dedicated to landing new clients. At the same time, you've invested $3,000 into a new contractor, employee, or outsourced service to remove all the low-value tasks off your plate.

Do you suppose you could land a new client if you dedicated sixty hours over a three-month period for that purpose specifically? I believe you could. So what's the value of adding a single new client? Is it $10,000? $20,000? $100,000? More?

Looking at it from that perspective, with that mindset, you can see how investing $3,000 over three months is well worth it. It's an investment with great ROI potential. Wouldn't you agree? If so, why aren't you already doing it?

Don't look at it as a cost. Look at it as an investment. If you keep putting it off because you want more revenue, or another client, or more experience, it will probably never happen. And the truth is, you're holding yourself back. Low-value tasks are a hindrance to the growth of your business.

Often, the real reason consultants want to keep doing all the low-value tasks themselves is because they are convinced they can do them better than anyone else. They know their own business, they know the market better, and they know what they want. All of those things might be true, but they are also—let's be frank—the ego talking.

If that's your situation, bear in mind, you are a subject matter expert, not a task expert. There are people out there who can put together a spreadsheet or a PowerPoint presentation for $50 an hour much better than you can. Why? Because it's their area of expertise. They will get it done far more efficiently than you.

In the end, you're not saving any money by holding onto all those menial tasks. You are costing yourself. Every month that goes by where you waste hours on low-value tasks is another month of lost revenue. That's an opportunity cost.

If you really want to grow your business, if you really want to increase revenue, then commit to doing what it takes to make that happen.

Adopt a mindset of investment rather than cost. There are people out there for every low-value task that you need to get done, and they'll do it faster and better than you. Let them do it. Spend your extra time doing the things that only you can do, adding the greatest value to your business, and concentrating on high-value tasks.

Ray Kroc is the man responsible for creating the McDonald's franchise model that turned the company from a single hamburger restaurant into a worldwide fast food chain. In order for the company to grow in those early years, someone had to make the hamburgers and pour the drinks, someone had to sweep the floor and throw away the trash. How silly would it have been if Ray Kroc had insisted on doing all of those things by himself?

"I can't hire someone else to grill the burgers! They won't know how to do it exactly the way I want it done."

Can you imagine him driving from franchise to franchise, trying to grill every burger, clean every bathroom, greet every customer?

"I have to do it all by myself. This is my business, and only I know what I really want."

Surely someone would have tried to talk sense to him eventually.

"Mr. Kroc, you have to hire some other people to do the low-value tasks. Get someone else to grill the burgers and clean the tables. You can't do it all by yourself."

"No, I can't. If I hire people, it will take time to train them. Plus, I'll have to pay them, and that's money I could put into my bank account instead."

If he'd done that, the company would never have grown. In fact, it would have folded within a month. Instead, from the very beginning, when it was still just a single location, he had a whole team of people making the food and taking care of the restaurant. He focused his efforts on selling new franchises and helping the company grow.

Larry Fink is the chairman and CEO of BlackRock, the largest money-management firm in the world. What if he insisted on doing all of the low-value tasks at the company by himself?

"I have to create all the paperwork. That means filling out every single form and application. I don't want anyone else doing that stuff because they won't do it exactly the way I want it done."

That attitude would make company growth impossible. In fact, it's an absurd notion. Larry Fink is surrounded by a vast team of people to handle all of the day-to-day operational and menial tasks that are necessary to keep BlackRock going. He focuses on high-value, big picture stuff.

Bill Bain probably didn't spend his time filling out spreadsheets and invoices at Bain & Company. Those things had to get done, of course, but he had plenty of people to do them. He spent his time revolutionizing the consulting industry by focusing on longer assignments and higher-value clients, something he could not have managed if he'd filled his days with menial tasks.

That same principle applies to your consulting business. Your job is to pour all your energy into high-value tasks that bring in new clients and new revenue. Let others do the rest.

"But I'll have to train new people," you might say. "Getting a new person up to speed on exactly what I need and want will take time away from my business. It's not worth it."

If it's a one-time task, if you just need to update the text on your website once, or if you need to format a single document, then it's fine to do it yourself. Hiring and training someone to do a one-time task isn't worth it. But if it's work that will have to be done repeatedly, like regular website updates or bookkeeping, then it's worth the training time in the long run.

WHAT NOT TO OUTSOURCE

There is one area of your business that you should not outsource, particularly in the early stages of your business, and that's your marketing. It might surprise you to read that.

"But I'm not a marketing expert. That's not my area of expertise. There are whole companies devoted to marketing. Doesn't it make sense to get one of them to do it?"

The truth is, until you've built a solid foundation in your marketing, it's best handled by you. What goes into that foundation? Clarity on who your ideal client is, developing a value proposition and marketing message that garners attention and resonates with that ideal client, and figuring out the best approach and language for your marketing in order to create conversations with buyers.

Those are things you have to figure out yourself. Once they are in place, then you have a foundation that someone else can build on. At that point, it might make sense to scale up your marketing efforts and offload some of the activities to others. As long as the foundation is solid, an outsourced marketer or firm can work real magic.

What happens if you outsource your marketing too early? You end up bringing in someone who might not understand your specific market or message, who might not fully understand your expertise or the value you offer clients.

Most marketing agencies are really good at creating ads and helping you with the sales process, but they simply will not understand your business, your customers, your experience, or your value as well as you do. I'm not suggesting you have to figure all of that out by yourself. It's a struggle for many consultants, which is why we address it in the Consulting Success Coaching Program. However, before you can expect someone else to effectively market your business, you have to put a foundation in place.

In the early days of Kentucky Fried Chicken, Colonel Sanders didn't hire a marketing firm to promote his chicken recipe. He created the message, came up with a sales pitch, and figured out who his ideal client was – and he did it all himself.

That meant getting in his car, traveling across the country to various restaurants, and presenting his product in person, having real conversations with potential buyers. By all accounts, he was persistent and a powerful salesman, and it didn't take long for his message to spread from city to city.

When he finally brought in outside agencies, he'd already created an image, message, reputation, and product that resonated. All the marketers had to do was build on the foundation he'd laid.

So, when it comes to marketing, spend time up front, in the early stages of your business, laying that foundation and putting it into practice. But offload those low-value tasks as soon as possible.

MINDSET REVIEW

- Don't wait to hire more people or bring in additional resources to help grow your business. You can't do everything by yourself.

- Assign low-value tasks to others, so you are free to focus on the high-value tasks that bring in new clients and revenue. It's an investment with great ROI potential.

- You are a subject matter expert, not a task expert. Don't hold onto menial tasks. There is an opportunity cost for doing so.

- In the early stages of your business, don't outsource your marketing. Until you've built a solid foundation in your marketing, it's best handled by you.

14

SIMPLIFY YOUR WAY TO SUCCESS

"Michael, I already know all of the strategies and tools available to consultants," Sal said, a spoon clutched in his hand. The residue of a hotel restaurant breakfast sat on a plate in front of him. "You have no idea how much time I've spent taking courses and webinars."

"That's great," I replied. "And have all of those courses and webinars created the results that you desire for your business?"

Sal cleared his throat, glanced down at a crust of bread on his plate, and tapped his spoon against the table.

"Well, no," he admitted. "Not yet."

He looked up at me again. The restaurant was large and airy, and cool air swept through the room from the expansive lobby just over his shoulder. We'd found a quiet corner, so we could speak openly.

"But, Michael," he continued. "My partners and I have thirty years of experience each. We are not new to consulting. We've had tremendous success in the past. We've tried everything."

"Everything?" I said, swirling the dregs of my coffee.

"I've set up funnels and sales pages," Sal said, speaking in a rush. "I have plenty of content. I'm ready to run webinars for the company. We have world-class connections throughout our industry. Heck, we ran a conference with fifty executives in attendance just a couple months ago." He finally paused to take a breath.

"Is it possible you've been trying to do too many things at once?" I said.

"What do you mean?" he replied.

"Maybe you've been trying to do so many different things that you are unable to give enough focus and attention to any one particular area," I suggested. "And maybe that is hampering your efforts."

Sal drummed his fingers on the tabletop. "I suppose it's possible. I'm not sure."

Like many independent professionals, Sal believed that in order to succeed he needed to do as much work as possible. He immediately adopted any new technology or tool that came along, poured his energy into anything hot and trendy. As a result, he was worn out, trying to juggle a dozen different things, and not seeing commensurate results.

The mindset behind this is understandable. More is better, right? That's what many cultures believe. Accumulating wealth and material possession is a sign of success, after all, so the principle must apply across the board.

The more you have, the more you succeed. Isn't that right?

No, actually, it's dead wrong. In fact, as I've experienced in my own business and working with hundreds of consultants through our Consulting Success Coaching Program, less is actually more.

You don't need an endless array of tools, technology, products, people, infrastructure, and office space. More of these things will not increase your chances of success, and, in fact, having too many might put you at a disadvantage.

Sometimes, I talk to clients who are disappointed because they've read a book or taken a course, and they feel like they didn't get much out of it.

"How many new ideas did you learn that you could implement?" I ask.

"Just one. I was hoping to learn so much more."

But one new idea, one new approach, or one new tool can be transformational. One valuable new idea makes the cost of the book or course a worthy investment many times over.

"Stop trying to learn everything," I say. "You don't need a hundred new ideas. You need one good one. Start putting it into practice."

It doesn't take much to create a million or even multi-million-dollar business. You can get there with just one product or service, one market focus, one way to market, one message, one delivery model, one business model, and one to three offers (variations on your product or service).

SIMPLIFICATION AND SUBTRACTION

If you adopt a strategy of throwing a whole bunch of stuff at the wall and hoping something sticks, the result will be messy and less than optimal.

The more tools, tech, and infrastructure you have, the more time it takes to learn and manage them all. The more products or services you offer, the more messages and value propositions you have to create and test. Then you have to layer a marketing and delivery system on top of each one, and the variations pile up.

Suppose you are targeting three markets at the same time with your offers. Everything being equal, your impact, energy, and focus can only be thirty-three percent for each one. Compare that to an individual who is hyper-focused on a single market. That consultant is free to commit a hundred percent of his energy and focus on that one market.

Who has the greater chance of making progress, increasing visibility, building a reputation as an authority, and winning more business? The individual giving thirty-three percent focus to three markets or the individual pouring a hundred percent of his energy and focus into just one?

I can give you the answer from experience. I have started, grown, and sold multiple businesses over the last eighteen years. The most successful ones, by far, including Consulting Success, achieved their success through a narrow focus, by simplification and subtraction rather than addition.

There is tremendous power in asking yourself, "What could I remove that isn't working, so that I can focus on the things are working?"

Why is it that some people are able to produce so much more than others in the same amount of time? It's because they are extremely focused.

McKinsey & Company is one of the most acclaimed and prestigious management consultancy firms in the industry, with revenue of over $8 billion. Why don't they also offer to do taxes or accounting for companies? They could, but it's not their focus. If they began pouring energy into those things, it might take away from what they're good at, what they're known for, and what they've built their reputation on.

A NEVER-ENDING CYCLE

In my own business, I am confronted with new marketing opportunities every single day. People want to partner with us constantly. I have friends who have seen great success through public speaking, YouTube videos, and Facebook Live. I could get involved in all of those things. But it's up to me to maintain focus.

There are countless ways to grow a business, and there's no end to new ideas, tactics, and tools. Many of them sound exciting, and they show great promise. It's easy to start dreaming about the impact they might make on your business.

"What if this new approach really works? What if this is the thing that finally produces our big breakthrough?"

Before you know it, you've purchased the book and signed up for the new service, and now you've added another thing into your busy schedule that you have to maintain. You dive in with great potential and promise, but soon enough, your enthusiasm fades.

Why? Because just around the corner is another new tactic or opportunity to entice you. The next hot thing will appear on your radar soon enough, whispering in your ear, "I'm the one. Trust me. I'll bring you the success you've always dreamed of."

It's a never-ending cycle, and once you get caught up in it, you feel like a hamster stuck on a wheel that can't get off.

Does this sound familiar?

It does to me. I spent years throwing money into each shiny new thing that came along, pouring energy into every new tactic or technique, fingers crossed for the breakthrough. I got carried away with all of these marketing dreams, but the more time I spent in this cycle, going around and around, the less progress I made.

Though the tech and tools and tactics piled up, my business wasn't thriving. Finally, one day, I was sitting down to dinner with my wife, and she could tell I was in a hurry. I had so little time to eat.

"Michael, do you really need to be doing so many things at once?" she asked, as I tried to speed my way through the meal.

"What's wrong with running three different businesses?" I replied. "I'm diversifying."

But as I continued to shovel in the food, I thought about her question in greater depth. Knowing my wife, she wasn't really looking for an answer. She was expressing a concern. As I considered it, I realized why progress in my businesses had been so slow: I was trying to do too much.

Within four months of that dinnertime conversation, my business partner and I had sold one of the businesses and later put a full-time manager in charge of another. That allowed me to focus all of my energy solely on Consulting Success, which, as a result, has grown exponentially and achieved tremendous success.

Getting to that point wasn't easy. Even today, I am constantly enticed by new opportunities all around me, and I have to consciously reject them, knowing they are additions that will take energy away from the things that really matter. Now, I get to help other people do the same thing. One of my clients, Leonor, saw greater success once she started focusing on the rights things. She doubled her average project value while running her business in a more simplified and focused manner.

As she put it, "I feel so much more focused, and my team tells me they've noticed a big difference, too. I have a lot more clarity around what I need to be doing each and every week with my marketing."

A CLEAR PLAN

Every new opportunity promises to add value to your business, and there are many things that can help your business grow. However, if you really want to make progress, you must have a clear plan in place that focuses on the following areas:

- Identifying your ideal client
- Having a way to get in front of your ideal client (marketing)
- Delivering a message that resonates with your ideal client

- Creating enough meaningful sales conversations each month to hit your target revenue
- Developing compelling offers at premium fee levels
- Serving and delivering value for your clients

Once you have that plan in place, stick with it. That's your focus. I'm not suggesting that every part of the plan is written in stone. If you need to change something, if you learn that your initial approach doesn't work, make appropriate adjustments. But avoid adding new ideas to the plan, and avoid jumping around.

"Are we moving forward and making progress on our plan?"

That's a question I ask myself every week, and it has contributed millions of dollars to my business by keeping us on track. It's that focus and clarity with our plan that enables me to quickly filter out new ideas and opportunities that aren't worthwhile.

Any time I am presented with a new opportunity, I ask, "Does this truly align with our plan, or is it an addition? Is it necessary or merely nice to have?"

You must do the same. If you want to achieve success faster, you have to simplify, remain fully focused and committed to your plan. Avoid any additions, and leverage the power of subtraction.

MINDSET REVIEW

- You don't need an endless array of tools, technology, products, people, infrastructure, and office space in order to succeed. In fact, it might put you at a disadvantage.

- You can succeed with just one product or service, one market focus, one way to market, one message, one delivery model, one business model, and one to three offers.

- Most successful people achieve their success through a narrow focus, by simplification and subtraction rather than addition. Simplify, remain fully focused and committed to your plan.

- Avoid adding new services or engaging in new marketing tactics just because they seem to be popular with others and are the latest shiny object.

15

YOUR PRESENT CREATES YOUR FUTURE

How many times would you have to fail hard at something before you stopped trying? How many mistakes would you have to make before you said, "I'm never going to get this right. I might as well give up."

Stephen King's first novel, *Carrie*, was rejected thirty times before it found a publisher. In fact, at one point, he threw the only copy of the manuscript in the trash, but his wife fished it out and made him keep trying. He just edges out Dr. Seuss, whose first book, *And to Think That I Saw It on Mulberry Street*, was only rejected twenty-seven times.

Robert Pirsig has them both beat. His New York Times bestseller *Zen and the Art of Motorcycle Maintenance* was famously rejected by more than a hundred different publishers before someone recognized its potential. It went on to sell five million copies.

What if Dr. Seuss had said, "The last publisher rejected me, so surely the next one will reject me? I might as well stop trying and do something else." What if Stephen King hadn't had a loved one to keep him going? If so, nobody would know their names today.

THE POWER OF THE PAST

The problem is, many people hold the belief that their past experience determines their present success.

It's a dangerous and inaccurate idea. If you believe your past experience determines your present success, you will continue doing what's worked for you in the past. That means you'll be less likely to consider newer and better opportunities for growth and development.

If, on the other hand, you've had some failures and disappointments in your past, you'll dismiss any similar opportunities that come your way, because your instinct will tell you, "I've already tried that. It doesn't work."

Both of these responses are unfortunate because they rely on an expectation that things always work out the same way, that history always repeats itself without change. This attitude is common among consultants, especially in regard to important business decisions like signing up for a new service, hiring a coach, or implementing a marketing strategy.

Let's say a consultant hired a coach in the past, and it wasn't a good fit or the results were disappointing. In the future, when they have an opportunity to hire another coach, they will be less likely to do so. They will measure the new coach by the disappointment of the old one. In reality, some coaches are simply better than others, and some have particular knowledge of your industry. The same goes for services. A service you've used in the past might not have worked out because of mistakes by the provider or because of a lack of proper implementation or follow-through.

How you view and deal with past failure has a huge impact on your future success. It can become your primary hindrance to growth.

SUCCESSFUL FAILURES

Nobody wants to fail. It's safe to assume Stephen King didn't enjoy having his first novel rejected thirty times. No consultant wants to be turned down by a client or discover that advice from a coach didn't work.

The possibility of failure is always scary, and the consequences leave scars on your pride and ego. That's why so many people work so hard to avoid failure at all costs. To do that, they stay as far away from sources of failure as possible.

"I tried that before, and it didn't work," becomes the mantra as they dismiss the next opportunity and move on.

Successful people don't let the mistakes of their past define their present performance. Instead, they focus on what works and keep striving toward their goals.

Babe Ruth held the home run record in Major League Baseball for thirty-four years, but he also held the record for strikeouts during that same period of time. If he'd had the wrong mindset, he might have defined himself by the strikeouts. Instead, he concentrated on the home runs, and it's what made him famous.

Consider the career of Michael Jordan. He's one of the most famous basketball players in the history of the sport. From winning Olympic gold in 1984 and 1992 to his six national NBA Championships, he had a stellar career. But along the way, by his own admission, he missed more than nine thousand shots and lost more than three hundred games.

Imagine if, after his first big loss, he'd said, "I'd better not play the next game. I lost the last one."

Instead, he famously said, "I have failed over and over and over again in my life. And that is why I succeed."

J.K. Rowling put it this way: "It is impossible to live without failing at something, unless you live so cautiously that you might as well not have lived at all, in which case you have failed by default."

Winston Churchill gave this particular insight: "Success consists of going from failure to failure without loss of enthusiasm."

Henry Ford founded one of the most famous automotive companies in the world, but not before he failed twice. His first two attempts at creating a successful business resulted in embarrassment. The first one, which he started in 1899 at the age of twenty-six, was called the Detroit Automobile Company. It didn't last long. Ford was never able to get the prototype car in good enough condition to sell, and the company disbanded. He tried again in 1901, creating the Henry Ford Company, but he left the company after a few months because of a bitter dispute with his financial backers.

The funny thing is, nobody remembers those first two companies. They only remember his third, the one called Ford Motor Company, the business that revolutionized the auto industry and pioneered the assembly line. Henry Ford went on to make one of the most popular cars in the world, the Model T, and his company continues to this day.

With the wrong mindset, he might have said, "I can't start another company. I've already tried it twice, and it doesn't work." But Henry didn't think that way.

What all successful people have in common is a view that failure is only a learning experience. They've become numb to the poison of failure.

When the average person gets knocked down, they scurry away to safety so it won't happen again. When a successful person gets knocked down, even if it happens multiple times, they get back up, make adjustments, and continue pushing forward.

Imagine an average person trying to play a professional hockey game. He's driving the puck down the ice when suddenly he gets body checked. An opposing player slams him hard into the glass. It's a bone-jarring hit, and he crumples to the ice, out of breath and in pain.

What does the average person do after that? Most likely, he limps off the ice, whimpering, and never attempts to play professional hockey ever again. When his friends ask him about it later, he might even avoid talking about it. He remembers it as an embarrassing moment in his life.

By contrast, a professional player makes every effort to absorb the pain, get up, and return to the game. That willingness to get up and keep trying is a big reason why he's made it to the professional level of his chosen sport.

Abandon the idea that failure is bad. Start to see every challenge, every taste of failure, as a way to learn, grow, and move closer to success.

Appreciate it. Benefit from it. Use it to your advantage.

So you got knocked down? Once you have the courage to get back up and keep moving, you've got the advantage.

MINDSET REVIEW

- Your past experiences don't determine your success. The choices you make and the actions you take today do.

- Don't dismiss an opportunity just because you've had disappointments in the past. That goes for services, coaches, and marketing strategies.

- Successful people don't let the mistakes of their past define their present performance.

- Start to see every challenge, setback, or failure as a way to learn, grow, and move closer to success.

.

16

MIRRORING SUCCESS

When I first started my consulting business with my business partner and cousin Sam, we had this wild dream of making $5,000 a month and being able to work anywhere in the world. It seemed like we'd never get there. We worked hard in those early months to win clients and grow, suffered some major setbacks, overcame numerous challenges, but eventually we reached that goal. It was an incredible feeling.

"Wow, $5,000 a month," Sam said. "Do you suppose we could reach $10,000?"

"Yeah, I don't see why not," I replied. "Let's make it happen."

What we were doing seemed to be working, so we kept at it. Growth was steady, and we were happy with the progress. Within a few months, we'd reached $10,000. Not long after that, we got into the range of $15,000 to $20,000 a month. We'd come a long way, grown tremendously, and we were excited.

But then something happened. Growth stopped. We reached a plateau. We were working harder than ever, pouring our energy into all of the things that had brought about success, but we couldn't reach the next level. We were stuck.

Have you ever been there? Are you there now, gazing up at the next level of business growth and wondering how to reach it?

Hitting a plateau in the growth of our business was discouraging, but we didn't give up. We had plenty of experience, we'd read countless books, and we'd accumulated a lot of ideas, but nothing was moving us to the next level. Something had to change. We needed a transformation.

It happened when I signed up for a coaching program along with other business owners. Most of these men and women were more successful than my cousin and I. By listening to their strategies and approaches to business, my mindset changed and our business model changed.

Within three months of taking the coaching program, our business went from $20,000 a month to $40,000, then $50,000, then $150,000 and beyond. The business model we'd had before had worked up to a point, but once it stopped working, it was time to change it. It was a $20,000 a month model, not a six-figure a month model. We had to learn from successful people in order to change the way we did things.

We didn't stop there, and we've never looked back. To this day, we invest in coaches and mentors to support our growth.

THE BEST INVESTMENT YOU CAN MAKE

Wherever you're at with your business, there is a higher level of success waiting for you. Never stop developing your mindset.

After all, what is the best place you can invest your money in order to get the greatest return? A high-interest savings account might provide you with a two percent return. That means your best-case scenario will probably only match the inflation rate. People who invest in the stock market jump for joy when they get a consistent return of twelve percent, and they're usually aiming for about ten percent.

Let's put that into concrete figures. If you invested $5,000 in stocks and achieved a twelve percent return every year for five years, you'd wind up with $8,811.71 at the end. That means, on average, you'd earn $762.34 each year on your investment. Not too shabby.

But what if I told you there's a way to invest that $10,000 and get a return of $30,000 or $100,000 or even $400,000? And what if you could get that return in less than a year? Sounds too good to be true? It's isn't. These kinds of returns are not only possible but common.

When you invest in your business by learning exactly how to grow, you will achieve similar results. Once you understand how to consistently attract your ideal client and how to increase your fees, you'll achieve a level of success that you've only dreamed about, and you'll do it quickly.

THE MIRROR EFFECT

In the end, the actions you take mirror your success to potential buyers. After all, you can't expect anything of others if you don't live it yourself.

If you want your clients to implement your recommendations consistently and with full commitment, make sure that you implement consistently and with full commitment. If you want buyers to respond to all of your communications quickly, make sure that you respond to all communications quickly. If you want clients to work with you on an ongoing basis, make sure you're committed for the long term; don't just dip in and out.

When you don't feel confident about your own expertise, when you are constantly comparing yourself unfavorably to others, buyers will sense it. When you lack confidence about the value you bring to the table, your clients will almost certainly notice the hesitation and lack of conviction in your tone of voice and body language.

Do you want buyers to invest with you at premium fees and see it as a great investment? Then view your own personal development as a worthwhile investment. If you choose not to get help from a coach or consultant to grow your business, how can you expect others to invest in you? If you take too much time making a buying decision, are overly conservative and cautious, or are indecisive, buyers will tend to treat you the same way, and you will begin to experience delays in your sales cycle.

Do you see how you are mirroring your own success to your potential buyers? It's all about aligning your actions with your desires.

MEANINGFUL SUCCESS

When you're considering signing up for a new service, conference, or coach, don't ask yourself, "Is this worth it?" Ask yourself, "Am I worth it?" It's not a cost but an investment in yourself. That subtle shift in thinking reflects a huge change in attitude, and it's the key to your success.

You can have years of experience in your domain, strong expertise, all the right skills, boundless energy, good connections, even good marketing, but if you don't develop a mindset of success, you will become the biggest hindrance to your business. You won't be able to realize your true potential.

That's why elite consultants constantly hone their mindset. They invest in themselves, improving the way they think and approach their business, so they learn how to deal with mistakes, frustrations, and fears. They know the right actions to take, and they have the confidence to take them.

Now it's your turn. I've given you the tools you need. If you will put them into practice, you, too, will unlock the door to meaningful, even limitless, success.

MINDSET REVIEW

- If you've hit a plateau in your business growth, your mindset and business model need to change.

- The actions you take mirror your success to potential buyers, so be confident in the value of your services. You can't expect anything of others if you don't live it yourself.

- If you want clients to implement your recommendations consistently, respond to communications quickly, and remain committed long-term, you must do the same.

- Never stop developing your mindset and sharpening your skills. An investment in yourself is the best investment you can make. It's the only investment where you determine the success and ROI you create.

CONSULTING SUCCESS COACHING PROGRAM

Consistently attract ideal clients, win high-value proposals, and scale your consulting business with confidence.

How effective is your marketing system in attracting clients?

You're a great consultant. You know how to provide value for your clients and help them reach their goals. However, if you're like most of the consultants we've worked with over the last 18+ years, your challenge isn't doing the client work, it's getting more clients. And most importantly, what you want is to attract ideal high-value clients on a predictable and consistent basis.

Sustainable and Profitable Growth

Many consultants find that referrals help them to get their first few clients. But referrals from your network don't always last.

In fact, the most successful consultants don't rely on referrals. They don't "rely" on anything. They take action. They master their marketing and sales. They build a system that predictably drives new leads and ideal clients. It's a system that once planned and built (the RIGHT way) becomes one of their highest points of leverage. It's what drives the growth of their business and makes it so profitable, consistent, and sustainable.

More Clients for Your Business

We help our clients and coaching students create these systems and they consistently get results. That's exactly what the Consulting Success Coaching Program is all about. We work with a small group of dedicated consultants and teach them how to consistently attract ideal clients, earn higher fees, win more proposals, and achieve meaningful success.

To learn more about the Consulting Success Coaching Program visit www.consultingsuccess.com

CONSULTING BLUEPRINT

At the time of printing, Consulting Success is offering a FREE 51-page Consulting Blueprint. You'll learn:

- How to develop a clear specialization that showcases your expertise
- Steps to attract ideal consulting clients
- Tips to improve your proposals and win more deals
- How to effectively structure your consulting offers
- And much more...

For instant and free access visit: www.consultingsuccess. com/blueprint

ABOUT THE AUTHOR

Michael Zipursky

Michael Zipursky is an entrepreneur, coach to elite consultants and CEO of ConsultingSuccess.com. He is a leading authority on marketing for independent consultants and consulting businesses, business growth, and pricing strategies. His clients include billion dollar global organizations, top consulting associations and elite independent consultants committed to meaningful success.

Michael has authored and co-authored numerous books on consulting including Consulting Success System, Masters of Consulting, Profitable Relations, and Creating Business Growth. His work has also been featured in MarketingProfs, HuffingtonPost, KISS Metrics, Maclean's, Institute of Management Consultants USA, Canadian Association of Management Consultants, and Chartered Management Institute in the UK.

In addition, Michael has coached and trained hundreds of consultants as part of his Consulting Success Coaching Program and over 6,000 consultants from around the world have taken his consulting courses and workshops.

Made in the USA
Coppell, TX
06 September 2022

82714906R00108